Beautifully Broken

ABIGAIL TENNANT

IMPORTANT INFORMATION

Should this book provoke any emotional distress please seek professional help. Samaritans are open 24 hours a day, 365 days a year, to listen to anything that is upsetting you. Call the national freephone number 116 123.

Copyright © 2018 Abigail Tennant
All rights reserved.
ISBN: 978-1726627306
ISBN-13

DEDICATION

I dedicate this book to my parents without whom I simply would not exist. I love you more than words can express. You have shaped me into the woman I am today and I am proud to have you both as parents.

Most importantly I dedicate this book to my children; you are my world and my saving grace. Whenever I feel lost I look to you for strength and each time I find it without you realizing.

I hope to be the best role model in your life and always inspire you to live your best life. I will forever shower you with love in each and every way possible. Keep dreaming BIG, crazy mammas got your back!

Table of Contents

DEDICATION 3

ACKNOWLEDGEMENTS 5

Chapter 1: Who Am I and Why Are You Reading This Book? 7

Chapter 2: Being grateful, starting now .. 23

Chapter 3: Breathe easy through life 40

Chapter 4: Be 'selfish' and take care of #1 (yes that's you) 57

Chapter 5: Life begins as you step out of your comfort zone 74

Chapter 6: Use your fear to soar 92

Chapter 7: Exercise the smart way 109

Chapter 8: Fuel your body to happiness 127

Chapter 9: Never Stop Learning 145

Chapter 10: The power of thoughts 163

Chapter 11: Dream bigger and bolder ... 180

ACKNOWLEDGEMENTS

THANK YOU

A huge thank you to all the likeminded people I have met in my journey of self-discovery.

To my two best friends, Claire and Rhiannon who have supported me to no end.

To my family who have supported me and my children from day one.

To Abigail and Sarah for their faith in me and making the process of sharing my passion more than just a dream.

Abigail Tennant

Chapter 1: Who Am I and Why Are You Reading This Book?

Who am I? Well hopefully you know my name and also my face after checking out the cover of this book.

Each time my 'Ice Breaker' changes slightly with experience. When it comes down to introducing myself it's actually one of the hardest things I do. I have so many 'strings to my bow' and so many goals I want to achieve. It's hard to define myself in a short sentence.

My coping strategy always used to be, give as little information I could get away with and move the spot light to the next person, to avoid my face heating up to a lovely bright red color.

Nowadays, I am an open book so here goes, a mini introduction and short version of my life story.

Explaining how I came to write this book and

become a motivational speaker and educator.

Hi, my name is Abigail, I am 32 and a mother of two amazing children. My daughter is 6 and my son is 4.

My childhood memories are not that clear, but I remember having a close family and spending quality time with my parents whether at home, on days out, or my favorite times on holiday in the caravan. All photos show me as a happy child so I go with that.

My school life looked ok to the outside, my parents saw a different side, although I covered most of it up. All my school comments were 'Abigail gets easily distracted'. I suppose that's how the bullying began. I was a push over in a sense. I was bullied from junior school all the way to secondary school and mainly by my 'friends'. I just wanted to be accepted so went along with it.

I was also the bully in some cases where I followed suit. I am not perfect and I am most definitely not proud, and sincerely apologise to anyone who I may have affected considering how bad it made me feel.

It made me realise though that most bullies have someone bullying them and it's a vicious cycle. I know my bullies were victims of bullying too. I wish I never felt the need to follow the crowd to fit in, I never once succeeded either.

On leaving school I went to college with a whole new group of people and completed a Level 2 in Beauty Therapy. However, due to a phobia of not knowing what client would be in front of me, I decided that it would not be the job I could see myself in. Instead I ended up working in retail and switched between a few jobs as I was not happy and went for more money as I was young and I followed the money.

I went on to work in hospitality then to food and beverage, followed by a nightclub which was one of my favorite jobs. I quit the bar work to take an opportunity to work in Dubai (not a popular destination at this point and, to give you a time scale Michael Jackson was staying with the prince of Dubai at the time).

I was going to work for Harvey Nichols but due to an unfortunate incident only a week into my arrival I returned home. A man, whom I assumed was an inspector came to my apartment which was controlled by security, so I had no concerns at the time in believing him.

He spoke another language so I could not understand and I was a naive 19 year old at the time. He then acted inappropriately and I managed to get him out of the apartment.

Thankfully the staff, security and police were straight on to the matter and it was dealt with immediately. However, on telling my parents I knew the best option was to return home. On coming home I managed to get myself a job back in the nightclub but most of the staff I worked with had left and it was not the same so I didn't stay. I then worked in a restaurant and again due to not feeling it was for me, I quit.

By then I was 20 and still no closer to figuring out what I wanted out of life, so when a family member suggested going on a little holiday I jumped at the chance. Sadly one day into the holiday I was subjected to being sexually assaulted and this really knocked my confidence. It was also the beginning of me fully covering up how I felt after telling one person, and I was told to stop being silly and get over it.

I felt humiliated, embarrassed and blamed myself massively for getting into the situation and not being able to get out of it. It was one of the most horrific experiences I have ever faced and one no one should ever have to experience, but one that young girls should be educated on, to show the dangers and how easy it is to get into a situation like I did.

All for being a friendly person and again still naive. My self-worth was almost gone but I met a really nice man and his son who became my saviors and allowed me to avoid being drawn back in the same situation.

Coming home I told no one and carried on being me like nothing had happened. I never told another person for a few years and only because I had come to terms with the fact it was not my fault and I was no longer ashamed. I went straight back into work and got a job in a call center and this was another great job.

I loved the people I worked with and built a good network of friends. Sadly the contract I was working on ended and we all got split up. I went to work in another contact center, and then another due me relocating back to my parents.

Things just kept going wrong. I was beginning to lose myself, and now looking back I realise I was sinking into depression. I did not want to go out, did not want to talk to anyone and became withdrawn. I just went to work and even that was not going too well, with the odd sick day when I could not face turning up.

At the age of 22 I began searching around on the internet to find what it was I wanted in life. I came across psychology and began to explore it, eventually I decided I wanted to become a psychologist as I was really interested in how the mind worked.

I put steps in place and I quit my job as they would not accommodate to me going back to college, and I was getting fed up of the people there too. I enrolled in the local college to do an 'Access to Higher Education' course after I got D in Math and Science but needed higher marks to get in to university. I worked in a working men's club evenings and weekends which I thoroughly enjoyed until the proprietor and his wife retired and it just was not the same. (You may notice I am a people person and if I don't get good vibes I remove myself from them. That being said those who I do like end up sliding out of my life somehow.) I did really well at college and this spurred me on to know there was a brain in me after all.

I went to a few universities and drove to Nottingham on my own to suss out if it was the place for me, I felt it was, and I was fortunate to be accepted to Nottingham Trent University, so I must have done something right. Sadly (and now becoming a pattern), it never worked out due to financial reasons so I had to withdraw my place. It was at this point I met the man who was to become the father to my children.

Now I was 23 and knowing I was not going to University I knew I needed to get a job. My friend told me of a full time job in a finance office where she worked. I got the job and I was pretty good at it, plus I had the best team leader which meant I enjoyed going to work. I then felt after two years that I wanted more but I was content with the company and it had been the longest I had stayed in one job.

Out of frustration that I was not progressing I replied to an email from the company director advising on how I agreed with his philosophy, and asked how could I move up in the company. Everyone was gob smacked! However I had the attitude of 'he emails us and he is just another human being'.

My email was polite and I did not regret it. He did in fact email me back much to everyone's surprise, and I began speaking with some people about making more of my enthusiasm for progression within the company, this dwindled and I was left chasing the wind. In the mean time I became a fitness instructor and began to follow the Zumba craze after work.

A job in the company was then advertised for a regional administrator, for which I applied and to my surprise I got the job. Not long into the role which was an eye opener and I will say no more, I found out I was pregnant with my daughter. I was 25 at the time but it was a shock to the system, although I had always been maternal and helped look after my niece and nephews, so I was excited to be a mum.

A week before Christmas I gave birth to my beautiful 10lb .1oz baby girl and I could not have been happier. At the time I was living with my parents but I wanted to get us a place of our own. I went back to work but returned to my old role.

I began looking for somewhere to rent, but also purchase if possible. It was my nephew who told me I should buy a new build house and for a laugh we went in and I pretended like I was in a position to buy a house, knowing I would never get a mortgage on my own. (This is where the law of attraction comes in which I will talk about later).

I went along with the paper work and even had a mortgage advisor come to see me. Turned out with the help to buy scheme and some help on the deposit I had actually gone and bought a home all by myself!!

The move then meant I stopped teaching due to relocation, but hey I now owned my very own home. We were now a little family of three, but the relationship was not working out very well and having a child just added more frustration.

I knew I did not want to be away from my daughter for long periods and went to work part time. Skip a few years and I felt broody but despite the relationship not being that strong I selfishly wanted another sibling for our daughter.

As luck would have it I fell pregnant at 27 with my son who came out at 9lb.12oz. For this birth I turned to hypnobirthing and it was the best thing I ever did, it even made my relationship with their father better as he was more involved. The birth was so quick and relatively painless. This is when I began to work on my breathing as a coping strategy for everything.

After having my son I knew for sure I did not want to return to work so I quit. I decided I would go back to the beginning and back to beauty now I had overcome my fear of what state the client would arrive in. I went back to college and completed my level 3 in beauty therapy and massage.

Despite being older than all the class (bar one but she left) I felt the girls welcomed me very well and I am still in touch with most of them albeit it over social media, they don't want me cramping their style.

I then became an apprentice and I was so thankful and worked with an amazing business owner. I was now being paid and this was a relief after having a house and bills, not to mention two children.

After completing college I felt I wanted more flexibility and did not want to mess around the business owner, so I left to become self-employed. With the help of the Princes Trust I was able to get backing to fund my business.

I went to work within a gym where I also qualified in level 2 Gym and level 3 personal training. It was at this point the relationship to the children's father broke down, just before my final exam which I somehow managed to pass despite having a mini breakdown in the car on the way.

The working environment at the gym was not for me and I left to go into a hair salon which only lasted a few months until she went bankrupt, only advising me a week before hand.

I attempted to keep going, working mobile and from home but it proved difficult. With the help and support of my princes trust mentor I was able to keep my head up and stay strong. The way in which my relationship ended was not the easiest but shortly after a web of secrets was exposed.

This was the worst period of my life and it was more difficult because I was trying to be mum to my two beautiful innocent children. So to say my world was falling apart I would say just about sums it up. It's hard to comprehend when you know there has been so much going on for a long period of time and you were unaware.

The wave of mixed emotions was more that I could handle, I felt trapped in a never ending roller-coaster and I desperately wanted to get off. My children however were my saving grace.

I had ironically, prior to the split, met a lovely group of ladies through a network marketing business opportunity. They were all involved in the business and were massively into this thing called 'Mind Set'. It was all new to me but I was intrigued (I will cover more later on mindset later in the book).

On top of this I was in a financial crisis. Instead of burying my head in the sand of debt I managed to get a part time job in a call center and met some amazing people. I was putting on the biggest, bravest face and performance of my life. I have new hair, new clothes and I made myself up every day.

Here no one knew me so I could be who I wanted. It was all going great at work, my new mindset was working. However, behind the scenes my life was a mess. I was over thinking and driving myself insane. I hardly slept and I only did after I cried myself to sleep. I woke up and the show would begin again.

It's hard to keep moving on when the one person that has caused you such pain is still a part of your life. Now don't get me wrong I was also to blame for the breakdown of the relationship. Although it's not a story for this book and it has two sides, so I feel it's unfair to go further into detail in this book.

My performance of coping and being 'OK' behind a false smile was not to last long, and I ended up in hospital with a suspected stroke which thankfully it was not. Instead it was put down to a neurological condition. I was also diagnosed with anxiety and depression.

My body was trying to tell me something. It was at this point I decided to get help and sought out Cognitive Behavioral Therapy (CBT).

Through what I know now, I believe I have been suffering with poor mental health and social anxiety ever since school as a result of indirect bullying. It would be hard for anyone to have noticed due to the front I put on, but there were a few who had seen me for the hermit I truly was. Especially my family who knew all I did was sleep, which was my escape from reality.

It is said that it takes a life changing event to often trigger mental health conditions and I was facing the hardest time of my life. Having trained and worked in both the beauty and fitness industry I have gained a lot of knowledge along the way on wellbeing. I re-evaluated my life using my knowledge and began to think in a new way, a positive way. I wanted a holistic way of healing not medication and I have never looked back.

What I have learnt in the last few years has been life changing. I have continued to face so many challenges that should break my spirit, but each time I bounce back faster and stronger. I am so much more aware now.

With this new found power and love for a better life I quit yet another job. This time taking a big leap of faith and I became a full time student at the ripe old age of 31, in what fate had been putting in my path so many times before, Psychology. I am now due to begin my second year.

Most people were against my decision but knew that once I set my mind to something I am doing it, even if it does not work out. I would rather try and it not work out than never try and wonder 'what if'. I proved everyone wrong and despite being a single mum to two children, one in school, one in nursery, living one hour commute from my chosen university and having a house and bills... I passed my first year first time.

Not only that but I was an active course rep too. Going to university has been the best thing I could have ever done. I have met the most amazing people and most of all my best mate and rock at university Rhiannon. I put myself forward for the department rep for the Psychology department and I got the place which is both an honor and a privilege. I am now proud to be a positive practitioner and ambassador for Snapp Happy.

I volunteer alongside Beanstalk as a reading helper with children. I have an amazing placement in place. I am trained with Mind in mental health awareness and I plan to work closely with my university, staff and students to improve wellbeing on campus and the North East of England alongside being the Vice President of the Mental Health Awareness Society.

I always take on a lot and I would not have it any other way. It keeps my mind active and occupied so it can't go off on its own destructive path.

Why read this book? Well if you want to begin living your best life this is the book for you. After all I have gone through I truly believe I am a better person and I want everyone to know, that no matter what issues they face in life it is possible to come out the other side with a positive outlook. It sounds crazy but I can see the positive in almost all situations and it's thanks to the lessons I have learnt along the way. I want to share my knowledge with you.

It is a widely known fact that mental health issues affect 1 in 4 people at any time in their life. I am one of the four. It is this reason that I wanted to write this book to help those who may be feeling a little lost. I never knew I had any issues with my mental health until I experienced a breakdown and began readdressing my life.

I wish someone had spoken more openly about mental health so I could have stopped hiding behind a joke and a smile to prove to everyone I was ok. I wish someone was able to tell me what I know now. The truth was I was a mess inside my own head, feeling trapped inside a body which often felt alien to me. Now I am happy being me, I am enough, I am strong and I am most definitely more beautiful for being broken.

The concept for the title of this book, 'Beautifully Broken' came as I searched for something that showed I was a better person, and a better version of me because of the drama I have faced in the most recent years of my life, which have forced me to reevaluate and find out who I really am, and who I want the world to see me as. I came across the ancient Japanese art of Kintsugi. For over 500 years the Japanese have restored their broken crockery through Kintsugi, otherwise known as 'golden joinery'.

The craftsmen would repair broken pieces with lacquer mixed with gold, silver or platinum. Showing off the broken pieces instead of throwing it away and buying new. It instead shows the history of an object rather than disguising it. Learning to embrace the flaws is something we should translate into life. I feel this is what I have done.

This book shares some of the ways I have been able to grow stronger than ever and become more beautiful for being broken. Using a broken vase as an analogy, the cracks in the vase are the times, events in my life that have left vivid memories, the missing pieces are parts of me that were lost such as confidence, self-worth.

On my journey to fix my broken vase I found golden wisdom which I used to repair the vase and fill in the gaps. Now my vase is restored and more beautifully broken.

Quotes

'The six best doctors: Sunshine, water, rest, air, exercise and diet.'
~ BUDDA

'First, think. Second, dream. Third, believe. And finally, dare.'
~ Walt Disney

'Learn how to be happy with what you have while you pursue all that you want.'
~ Jim Rohn

Chapter 2: Being grateful, starting now

'Gratitude is what starts the receiving process. Only by giving are you able to receive more than you already have.'
~ Jim Rhon

What is Gratitude?

Gratitude can be defined as:

The quality of being thankful; readiness to show appreciation for and to return kindness.

I have heard gratitude explained over and over again on my journey to finding true happiness. At first I thought I was grateful, therefore I overlooked the true meaning of 'gratitude'. The more I heard the word, the more I decided to really invest in the process and start small.

I began doing this as soon as I woke up and before I went to sleep, and found my day started better and the quality of my sleep improved.

But why?

Throughout history gratitude has been mentioned many times. The roman philosopher Marcus Tullius Cicero considered the act of gratitude to be the parent of all virtues. Now more than 2,000 years after his passing gratitude is becoming a global subject. A subject many are still unaware of.

My Queen of gratitude is Oprah Winfrey, who even insists that a 'gratitude diary' has been the most important thing she has done in her life. For years she has spoken passionately about the power and pleasure of being grateful.

It sounds so simple, surely we are always grateful for all we have?

Or maybe we overlook the things we have, on a search for all the things we don't have?

Philosopher William Penn said 'The secret to happiness is to count your blessings while others are adding up their troubles.' Concentrate on what you have already!

Buddhists have known for years the power of gratitude. Buddhism teaches that when negative emotion develops, it stops us being able to see reality. When a mind is filled with anger the chances are a wrong decision will be made, leading to regret. This has potential to turn into a destructive cycle. Instead they encourage individuals to keep a calm mind and not ignore their problems but look at them with a realistic attitude.

My favorite person who discussed gratitude is of course H H Dalai Lama. 'Every day, think as you wake up, today I am fortunate to be alive, I have a precious human life, I am not going to waste it. I am going to use all my energies to develop myself, to expand my heart out to others; to achieve enlightenment for the benefit of all beings.'

It has also been scientifically proven that being grateful is beneficial for our wellbeing. In a study by Emmons & McCullough 2002, they found improvements on the immune system.

Psychologists are hugely interested in this area, they suggest that gratitude and wellbeing are strongly related. Back in 1998 Martin Seligman, was the president of the American Psychological Association and used Positive Psychology as a theme for his term.

In a Ted Talk Seligman discussed one aim of positive psychology, which was the need to be as concerned with strength as with weakness. So Positive Psychology in everyday life means that instead of looking for the things going wrong, it is time to focus on what is going right in our life.

Harvard Medical School states, 'a thankful

appreciation for what an individual receives, whether tangible or intangible. With gratitude, people acknowledge the goodness in their lives ... As a result, gratitude also helps people connect to something larger than themselves as individuals- whether to other people, nature or a higher power.'

Through listening to 'The Secret' they found that there is no greater way of starting your day than by being grateful. Every teacher who is a part of the book uses gratitude as part of their day. By making a list of the things you are grateful for it begins to shift your energy and thinking. James Wray comments that he makes gratitude a morning routine.

Not only does he think about the things he is grateful for but he connects to the feelings of gratitude. Dr Joe Vitale talked about 'like attracts like', as soon as you start to feel the feelings of gratitude for what you already have, you attract more things you can be grateful for.

Who doesn't want to start their morning the right way?

I purchased a book by Hal Elrod called 'The Miracle Morning', which aims to transform your life before 8am. I am the kind of person who wants to see results quick and his Six Minute Miracle Morning was just what I needed.

In minute one he suggests 'a prayer of

gratitude to appreciate the moment' referring to waking up. Minute four is writing down some of the things you are grateful for. I use the full six minute guide and I make sure I get it done in peace by waking up and hour before my children. I am beyond grateful for that time to myself and I start my day right.

At first I was not too sure about this process, but how can so many people be wrong? My way of thinking is what have you got to lose by giving it a go? In the next section I explain just how much I'm grateful for what I have and appreciating what I have more of. It not only makes me feel better but I really do attract more things and people into my life that I am hugely grateful for.

My experience

I always remember as a child my parents would always make me aware of how grateful I should be and how not everyone was as fortunate as us. As a child I was brought up in a Christian church and learnt to be thankful.

I am blessed for this upbringing and although I no longer attend church or associate myself with a faith as such I do appreciate the morals and the belief I have taken from being surrounded by the church as a child.

I now send my children to a Church of England school to enable them to learn the same way I did.
I did not come from an affluent family which at the time did not bother me. However my parents never made me feel like money was an issue. My parents were wise with their money, and I don't blame them looking back now, and after all they had worked hard for it. I never saw them struggle or complain in relation to money.

We went on holidays and did fun things together. In comparison to some of my 'friends' we were well off in my eyes, although some of the other kids got designer and trendy clothes and footwear. My mum refused to spend excess money on material objects when there were other alternatives which were just as good quality and less money. She did not believe in paying extra just for the brand name. At the time I could not understand, we had money so why could I not get the same things.

I really wanted to fit in and this made me resentful and angry at times. As a result for not being 'on trend,' I was being bullied for not having the latest fashion. Surely we had money to stop me being a target? I used to cry to my mum and plead her to get me something.

She agreed once to get me some tracksuit bottoms, I was over the moon and I beamed from ear to ear in the sports shop and went over to the pair my 'friends' had. My mum redirected me to a cheaper pair, they were not the right pair! My mum only gave me one option, buy the 'wrong ones' or get nothing. Well I got them and thought it's better than nothing, but in the back of my mind I knew they were not going to be good enough. I went proudly as I could to school only to be mocked for getting the wrong ones. Yet again my soul was crushed.

On looking back now I totally appreciate what my mum did for me even though at the time I could not see it. I understand now her reluctance to spend more money than necessary on material things just because everyone else had them.

All my clothes were new and clean, I never needed the named brand. I wish I had the courage to stand up for myself and state that it was irrelevant what I was wearing. I now see

I should have just been more grateful that my mum had even considered buying me anything designer. I thought I appreciated what I had and only now do I see that because I wanted more of what I could not have, I could not even see what I already had.

By focusing on what I did not have, it made me have a negative outlook (the bullies never helped either). Having children myself now, I always remind them how fortunate they are and to see the bigger picture. I drill the lesson I needed to learn into them so they don't suffer the same fate as me. Hey that's what parenting is about right?

Teaching them the lessons you wish you had learnt quicker?

However, I only came to this realisation when I turned 29 and I was introduced to a marketing network business. That was when gratitude started to play a big role in my life. It was also a turning point in my mindset. I was working as an apprentice in a beauty salon while completing my level 3 in beauty therapy and massage.

I loved my job at the time but the wage was not much at all, bearing in mind I had a house, bills and two children to pay for. It was also the time my relationship to their father really began to break. So I decided to give network marketing a go in my spare time for some extra cash.

I had reservations throughout as I was not a social person and I did not know many people. I was already anxious when meeting new people so engaging them in the products I was promoting was a challenge. However, I knew I had to give it a go, I loved the products and did my research on the company so I had faith in what I was promoting.

Very quickly I realised that it was not just about selling, it was actually about working on yourself, your mindset and your belief in yourself.

I felt myself gaining more confidence and wondered why I had never come across mindset work before. I had heard about Positive Mental Attitude (PMA) but never mindset. So I looked at the definition of mindset which is: 'The established set of attitudes held by someone'. I looked to one lady in particular called Emma of whom I never met. I was totally in awe and felt strangely connected to her.

I began listening to what she had done to gain confidence. This was the beginning of my journey of self-development. She also mentioned gratitude and so I began daily gratification notes. I used affirmation statements to motivate and focus on a goal and recited them repeatedly to absorb into my subconscious mind.

I began listening to others who had changed their thought process, such as Tony Robbins,

Dave O'Connor, Jim Rhon and Robert Kiyosaki, to name just a few, they all mention gratitude. A few months in my mindset was changing for the better but I realised I was more focused on working on my mindset than I was about the business.

So I stopped working on the business and focused on working on me. Everything happens for a reason and this company was brought into my life to help change my mindset and establish positive thinking.

One book the group promoted amongst each other was 'The Secret by Rhonda Byrne'. As I struggle to read due to having dyslexia and Irlen syndrome, I downloaded it on audio. This is when I began to go for a walk/run while listening to audio books. I found every time I listened to the audio of 'The Secret' something new clicked each time and it was like a lightbulb being lit up so bright.

I found myself smiling so much and an overwhelming sense of empowerment for life. I appreciated things around me more, I fell in love with nature and being outside in the fresh air. I even began to run!! That's not like me at all, more over I actually enjoyed it! I would rush home and note down whatever had come into my mind. I was filled with enthusiasm and a whole new lease of life.

It is thanks to 'The secret' that I learnt more about gratitude. I began to appreciate all that I had at that moment and stop focusing on all the things I did not have. My focus changed. I became more aware of my present. I began to say thank you out loud for waking up to another day. I still do and always will.

When I began to be thankful for all that I had, I suddenly realised just how much I actually had! I had a lovely house with a big garden, a reliable car, a fully furnished home, heating, clean water, a full fridge, two healthy children, a supportive family, a handful of really good friends, and the list went on. I then looked closer and listed all I had achieved in life. Granted I did not do much with most of my qualifications but I achieved them none the less.

I then realised I had previously been spending so much energy focusing on the things I did not have. I found my new way of thinking and simply by being grateful my life was happier. I told people in my life just how grateful I was to have them in my life and why. I had more appreciation for those around me and especially my parents.

All this came from the power of gratitude and simply being grateful and appreciating all I had, and it cost me nothing. I continue to this day to be thankful for all the small things more than the big things. Sometimes it's the small things that get taken for granted and I don't want to live a life like that. It's the small things that keep you grounded.

Quotes

'Let us rise up and be thankful, for if we didn't learn a lot today, at least we learned a little, and if we didn't learn a little, at least we didn't get sick, and if we got sick, at least we didn't die; so let us all be thankful.'
~ Buddha

'The single greatest thing you can do to change your life today would be to start being grateful for what you have right now.'
~ Oprah Winfrey

'Feeling grateful and not expressing it is like wrapping a present and not giving it.'
~ William Arthur Ward

'Gratitude is riches. Complaint is poverty.'
~ Doris Day

Did you know?

> ➢ Stress hormones such as cortisol are 23% lower in those who show gratitude. The same people are likely to produce more oxytocin, the happy hormone.
>
> ➢ Writing down with pen and paper is proven to help your brain engage more.
>
> ➢ Being grateful improves physical health, as you are more likely to take care of yourself and appreciate your body.
>
> ➢ Grateful people sleep better.
>
> ➢ Being grateful helps keep you optimistic about your future.
>
> ➢ Gratitude has positive effects on the brain, including neurotransmitters and hormones.

Putting it into practice

- ❖ Keep a gratitude journal and when you feel in doubt look back over all the things you have been grateful for.

- ❖ On a morning when you wake before you get out of bed think of 3 things you are grateful for.

- ❖ Once you're awake write them down.

- ❖ Thank someone in your life and tell them why you're grateful for them, no matter how small.

- ❖ Open your eyes and be aware of all that is around you and all that you have.

Download your FREE daily positivity and gratitude sheet from www.attunedmindset.co.uk to ensure you start as you mean to go on.

What have you taken from this chapter?

....
....
....
....
....
....
....
....
....
....
....
....
....
....
....
....
....
....
....
....
....
....

What one thing will you implement going forward?

....
....
....
....
....
....
....
....
....
....
....
....
....
....
....
....
....
....
....
....
....
....
....

Notes

Chapter 3: Breathe easy through life

'Breath is the link between mind and body.'
~ Dan Brule

What is Breath Work?

The definition of breath is:
The air taken into or expelled from the lungs.

The definition of breathing is:
The process of taking air into and expelling it from the lungs.

You may be wondering why I have dedicated a chapter to something as simple as breathing. Well the answer is breathing is underrated, because it is something we do without needing to think about it.

The only time it's brought to our attention is if it drastically changes, such as when we experience fear, laughter, panic, when we cry and so on.

An interesting fact I learnt is that we can make our breath hot and we can make our breath cool. We do this instinctively. When we are cold we blown on our hands to warm them up, when we want to cool our food down we blow cool air on it. Pretty amazing if you ask me.

In order to breathe our body needs to follow a process, it does so without us needing to tell the body what to do. It's the first thing we do instinctively when we are born. We all breathe and we need to in order to survive. Our breath alters all day, every day to stay in tune with our body.

When we are laughing, crying, exercising, scared, excited, no matter what our breath works without us needing to think about it. It is only when it changes we need to become aware, and then know how to get back to breathing normally. Hence breath work is simply being more in tune with your breathing process.

Breath work is seen as consciously taking control, becoming more focused and more aware of your breathing. It also allows us to take control of our thoughts (we go into this further in the book).

Breathing is important because the cells in our body need a new supply of oxygen so they can be energised. Breath is the first thing we experience when we are born, and the last thing when we pass. It's vital for our survival.

So we know what 'breath' is and that breath work is focusing on our breathing but is that it? No, not quite. Have you ever been in a situation and someone says 'just breathe'?

Well we already established we all have to breathe to survive, however there are many types of breathing and some do us more harm than good. Such as calm breathing does us good and hyperventilating (over breathing) does us harm.

In my hunt for knowledge while attempting to start running, I looked at runners as my first port of call, in figuring out how they breathe as they focus on this element. In the past I suffered with panic attacks when my breathing became out of control due to lack of awareness.

According to 'Runners World' rhythmic breathing helps to keep runners injury free, so they match their breathing to when their foot lands on the ground, allowing the impact to be equal on both sides. In order to begin they suggest starting to learn to breathe from your diaphragm while lying down, which will help increase the volume in the chest cavity. Once this is established a pattern can then be introduced that works with your running style.

Interesting stuff, and if you're a runner I

would encourage you to explore this as it will improve your running if done correctly.

Then I looked at meditation to calm my mind and see if I could help myself focus more. Now, anyone who has heard about meditation will assume it's all about long deep breaths and humming/chanting. Well it is in some practices. In yoga they train you to connect with your breathing.

When you are connected you become present in the moment. This is also the reason breathing is an integral part of meditation too. In changing the pattern of your breathing you can produce different states of mind.

I then stumbled upon a great 'go to' guy called Dan Brule. I was drawn to him for a very good reason and I have learnt so much. The knowledge throughout his book called Just Breathe, (it is available on audio and is voiced by Dan himself) is extremely insightful as he draws on all aspects of breath work from a range of sources.

He discusses varies breathing exercises, techniques and meditation that he has studied, practiced and tested. It is a very interesting book that will change your perspective.

Through Dan alone my eyes were opened to just how many different ways we can breathe. Thought self-exploration you can see which techniques you decide work best for you. As I began to discover, explore and develop my breathing that I realised just how much power and potential there was behind something I once overlooked, even though it was right under my nose.

When I went to look beyond Dan's work, (he provided the names of other people in the field of breathing) I was drawn to Peter M. Litchfield. He did work on respiratory psychophysiology and states 'Reconnecting with one's breathing is the first step in the direction of self-healing and self-realisation'.

He produced a paper in 2003 titled 'A brief overview of the chemistry of respiration and the breathing heart wave' which I read. It is a very interesting read; if you want to educate yourself more on the science behind why focusing on your breath is so important if not vital.

It stated that the effects of over breathing negatively affected health, cognition, emotion and performance. The term 'heart wave' refers to the cycles of our heart rate otherwise known as 'heart rate variability' or 'HRV' should you wish to look into this further.

Hopefully I have shown just how important our breath is and it encourages you to become more mindful and investigate further for which links are available on my website: www.attunedmindset.co.uk

My experience

I first heard the term 'breath work' when I was pregnant with my son. On the way to prenatal appointment I noticed a poster for Hypnobirthing and I was intrigued. I enrolled and began the classes. I was advised it was beneficial to bring along your partner, I had a hard time convincing my children's father to join me for support.

He finally gave in and despite his reservations he learnt a lot and came with me to all the other classes. He recommends it to any father out there so they know what to expect and not just the mother of the child. I also highly recommend it even if you're skeptical as you have nothing to lose but potential to learn something new.

The course came with a book and cd to listen to. It was strange at first as I had never even tried meditation but I was open minded and went along with it. After reading about the process and the desired outcome, I invested my time and began working on my breathing from that point onwards. The results when it came to giving birth were amazing.

With every twinge I took deep calm breaths, I remember my sister rubbing my back and asking how I was managing to cope. She said I looked like I was in my own world, and I was. I was so focused on me, my breathing and of course my baby boy.

When the paramedics arrived to take me to hospital I was given the delights of gas and air but again I had to focus on my breathing to ensure I got the benefit of contents. By the time we got to the hospital I was almost ready to give birth and I was shocked at how well I was coping.

I have to admit I did end up getting some pain relief and it was only because I wrote it on the birth plan that I may want it (following the drama I faced with my first birth). I was too in the zone and I said yes when they asked but did not fully know what I had said yes to until it was too late.

By having the injection it actually slowed the birth down and I was really disappointed in myself. I had already gone almost all the way by just breathing. Never mind, should I have the good fortune to do it again I most definitely will not be having any drugs.

I never really had use for the breathing techniques after the birth, it was kind of put on the back shelf so to speak. However, when my son was around 9 months I decided to get back into fitness. Without realising it I began to use the breathing exercises while exercising and the only reason I noticed was because I felt in control and not out of breath or sweaty, which was strange for me.

I found it really helpful once I got my breathing right when I was working out, it helped me be in control. It also helps you to keep in tune with your body so you know your limits and in turn potentially avoid injury.

I then decided that I wanted to start running and knew I would have to control my breathing to avoid panic attacks from my childhood. I googled the hell out of it and read various tips. The main tip I would see over and over again was breath work and working to a 'pattern' that suited the runner.

It took some practice to work out what worked for me and I actually enjoyed practicing even if I did look a little strange, (I did not care, I was in my own little bubble). I also had my audio on so I was distracted from the fact I was running. I was simply listening and breathing.

Before I knew it I was running and it felt good, like really good, almost like I had achieved something really big. Well I had! I took baby steps and downloaded the Army App which had a voice guided coach and interval training which I found useful and worked over the top of my audio. I found running for me was just mind over matter, I no longer minded therefore it no longer mattered. Now I can go for longer periods without a break and I don't freak out.

I then went through my difficult time with all that was going on in my life, and I felt overwhelmed and drained. I decided I really wanted to give meditation a go and discovered the power of focusing on your breath. Through guided meditation I found it really helped me to sleep better which helped me to recuperate some energy.

Prior to my daughter I was a sleeping princess, fast forward to becoming pregnant and I have not had a decent night sleep since, although it is getting better as they get older and I get wiser. I have my motherly instinct that makes me listen out for my children, every noise I would go and investigate.

They on the other hand have a child instinct that knows when mummy is fast asleep so they choose that point to come and climb in with me, sleep sideways, touch me to make sure I'm there, smack me in the face with a head/hand/foot (accidently of course).

At one point they would take turns coming in and stand right next to me whispering 'MAM' loudly till I answered, then tell me they had a nightmare or they can't sleep. (Now I know how my parents felt when I did it!)

Depending on how tired I was I would either take them back to bed with a kiss, cuddle and reassurance it would be ok or ... let them in with me- with a reluctant sigh and a few deep breaths.

Anyway, back to breathing... Once I knew about conscious breathing, I used it as a way of focusing my mind to stop it wandering, as this impacted a lot on my sleep while going through the separation with my children's father and beyond.

Alongside my other tips to refocus my mind, the breathing helped massively. I found as I concentrated on my breathing, before I knew it I was asleep. Result! This got me thinking, and on my search for another audio I looked into books to help with breathing, relaxation, meditation and so on and I came across Dan Brule. (The law of attraction knew where to guide me.)

I downloaded Dan's audio book 'Just Breathe- Mastering breath work for success in life, love, business and beyond' (I re listen to this a lot, he is easy on the ear). I gained so much knowledge and began to have so much gratitude for my ability to breath, and my ability to learn. I followed a lot of his practices while on the beach, some of which made me laugh, especially the yawning exercise.

Basically, I was walking along the beach allowing myself to experience full yawn's with sound effects. It was so fascinating to learn about breathing. A vital component of life that we often take for granted. I now love to just go walking in the country or on the beach and just breathe!

Now that I can connect with my breath, I just feel so much more alive and in tune with my body. I take more in, I am more present. When I get stressed, I simply focus on my breathing. When I want to take a moment to think clearly, I simply focus on my breathing. When I feel emotional, I simply focus on my breathing. When I am faced with a difficult situation, I simply focus on my breathing and decide if it's worth my energy or not. My energy is precious and I want to spend it wisely.

Most of all, breathing has allowed me to become more aware of my feelings, and gives me the time to think about things logically rather than make a hasty decision. It allows me to be more patient, therefore helping reduce my stress and anxiety levels.

Who knew that breathing was so much more complexed yet so easy once you know how to do it with knowledge on why you're doing it in the first place?

Quotes

'Conscious breathing heightens awareness and deepens relaxation.'
~ Dan Brule

'Just breathing can be such a luxury sometimes.'
~ Walter Kirn

'Never underestimate the healing power of a long, deep breath. Not only does it create inner calm, it gives you space to acknowledge and appreciate that this breath is not your last one.'
~ Lori Deschene

'Our way to practice is one step at a time, one breath at a time.'
~ Shunryu Suzuki

Did you know?

- It is said on average if we breathe 15 times per minute we will live to 75-80 years. Reduce that to 10 times per minute and we live to 100.

- The body is said to be able to last 3 weeks without food, 3 days without water but only 3 minutes without air (unless you train to hold your breath longer).

- Without air the brain is starved of oxygen and the body is no longer able to function. It is something we take to easily for granted.

- If the lungs were open flat they would cover the entire size of a tennis court!

- The lungs are the only organs that can float on water.

Putting it into practice

- ❖ Set aside a 5 minutes, if you can make sure it is quiet and you have the opportunity to concentrate on your breathing. Simply start with a few long deep breaths, in for 4 out for 4 and increase if need be. Just do what feels comfortable for you. Focus on the rising and lowering of your chest. Listen to the sound of your breath and don't be afraid to make noises. Do the same this time with your eyes closed. Practice this for a few minutes each day.

- ❖ Bedtime breathing- ensure you are comfortable then close your eyes slow your breathing down slowly and begin to focus on your breath

- ❖ Become aware of your body. Begin with your feet and with every breath, breathe to the area clenching/squeezing and as you breath out let go and feel your body relaxing. Move to your legs, buttocks, abdomen, lower back, chest, upper back, shoulders, arms and hands. Now let go of all the tension in your face. Notice your eyes become heavy, all the while continuing to focus on breathing in... and out... you are now totally relaxed, now enjoy and sleep well.

Download your FREE daily breath work guide sheet from www.attunedmindset.co.uk to ensure you breathe happy.

What have you taken from this chapter?

What one thing will you implement going forward?

Notes

Chapter 4: Be 'selfish' and take care of #1 (yes that's you)

'To be successful you have to be selfish, or else you never achieve.'
~ Michael Jordon

What is Self-Care?

The World Health Organisation defined self-care in 1998 as:

Self-care is what people do for themselves to establish and maintain health, and to prevent and deal with illness. It is a broad concept encompassing hygiene (general and personal), nutrition (type and quality of food eaten), lifestyle (sporting activities, leisure etc.), environmental factors (living conditions, social habits, etc.), socio-economic factors (income level, cultural beliefs, etc.) and self-medication.'

However, self-care can be described in many different ways by each person you meet. It is one of those subjects where the definition is mainly down to the individuals interpretation.

The term itself, 'Self-care', has become a buzz word in society. If you switch the words around it may help, as you understand that it simply means caring about yourself. It is not a new term, as throughout history healthcare has focused on the issue and people were responsible for their own health.

It is only with time that the emphasis has changed. In the 19th century health care was revolutionized by science, medical discoveries and technological advances meaning we were putting our health in the hands of the professionals more.

This has lead society to lean on the health system to take care of us and the burden and strain is now taking its toll. When will we realise we need to be in charge of our own health and prevent illness as much as we can, only turning to the medical professionals when it becomes beyond our control.

Self-care is when we deliberately take time out to care for our mental, emotional and physical health and wellbeing. It is most definitely not a selfish act, more of a necessary one. Putting yourself as a priority should not be seen as selfish, but as a way of ensuring you can be there for others if needed, such as family and friends.

It allows us to refuel ourselves in what society has changed into, a very high paced and challenging living environment. Only you can choose to make changes.

So many people I know are suffering because they are putting others first and not taking care of themselves, and I see them running themselves into the ground. Now I am not saying I want them to forget about those who they care for but, in order to care for others effectively they need to be in the best health too.

The only way they can, is if they put themselves first. It sounds so harsh at first but think of when you get emergency instructions for example on an airplane, the advice they give is ensure you fit your oxygen mask first before helping others. I am sure I don't have to state the obvious but I will anyway... you can't help others if you're dying yourself.

Self-care does not need to be done in isolation either, it can be carried out by doing something you love with someone you love, friends or family, even strangers who may become friends. A good sleep is self-care, as your body needs rest to function at its best.

You can't expect it to function 24/7 without a break now can you? It won't do anyone any good. Aim to have at least one pleasurable activity a day and look for opportunities to laugh; laughter is good for your soul. Mind blowing right? Who's laughing now?

Speaking of laughter, have you ever had a belly laugh and not felt good. Your body automatically fills with the happy hormones: dopamine (reward), oxytocin (love), serotonin (mood) and endorphins (positivity).

Laughter can decrease stress and increase immune cells and infection fighting antibodies. I heard a story of a gentleman called Norman Cousins who was diagnosed with a crippling connective tissue disease which was referred to as collagen disease.

He was given a 1 in 500 chance of recovery and a relatively short amount of time to live. He decided to develop his own recovery plan and took massive intravenous doses of vitamin C and laughter through a show called 'Candid camera' and various comedy films.

He reported that he 'made the joyous discovery that ten minutes of genuine belly laughter had an anesthetic effect' that would give him 'at least two hours of pain-free sleep' and when the effects wore off he would put on another film and 'not infrequently, it would lead to another pain-free interval'. He went on to live for another 26 years, despite other medical conditions.

Or just watch Patch Adams for another example, with the amazing soul that was Robin Williams.

In taking care of yourself you are helping to prevent yourself from illness. Excessive drinking, eating too much junk food, smoking, missing vital Dr. appointments, the list can go on with the way we mistreat our body. Now that's not to say cut out all the things you enjoy, as I keep saying it's all about the choices you make.

It is always put to us to do things in moderation. All I am saying is make sure your more mindful about the choices you are making, and the potential effects they may have on your health and wellbeing.

I love finding meaningful quotes, (you may have noticed already) and so many refer to self-care. I often hear people say they are too busy to look after themselves, they have others they need to look after. Why is there guilt around taking time out to put ourselves first?

The charity Mind states that 'Self-care techniques and general lifestyle changes can help manage the symptoms of many mental health problems. It may also help prevent some problems from developing or getting worse.' At the end of the day we live in our body 24/7 so we need to look after every inch of it, mind and body. In order to do this we need to introduce... self-care!!

My experience

If someone asked me years ago 'do you take care of yourself?' I would have answered yes. Well I was clean, tidy, presentable and took some pride in my appearance (I only say 'some' as I never went overboard with the makeup, I was all for minimum effort.).

Now I know what self-care actually is I suppose I should have answered no. I never put my happiness as a focus and just went through life with not much focus on me as a person. I was a people pleaser and put their needs before mine.

Looking back I feel saddened that I did not like who I was and allowed others to 'walk all over me'. I was focused on what other people may think, I never loved myself at all. Being in my skin was not a comfortable feeling, I would sometimes stand in the shower crying and grabbing at my skin wanting to rip it off.

Hatred was the only word I could use for myself at one point. I would look in the mirror in disgust and talk negatively to myself saying how I hated myself and I looked a mess, how I was useless and nothing was ever going to work out. I would say I was fat, ugly, no one would ever love me, the list went on.

Negative self-talk on a whole new level. I could never imagine saying that to myself now and I get emotional thinking about it. I wish that someone had just told me that the more you say something the more it sticks, and that in order to change my thoughts I had to change my way of thinking.

I wish I could go back in time and place my hand on the shoulder of the old me and whisper, 'Stop being so hard on yourself. You are enough. You have so much potential'.

I am now a massive fan of self-care. I LOVE ME. At first I used to always rush my 'me time' and not actually enjoy the moment (I had kids at this point). I now love what I call a spa bath when I have time alone while the children are in bed.

It consists of a hot bubble bath, candles (safely of course), conditioning hair mask, face scrub and mask, body scrub and exfoliating mitt, relaxing music and cucumbers for my eyes. It's my time of bliss. I am not being mam or a student, I am just me.

I also have times where I do absolutely nothing. I don't feel guilty about it either. This took me a while to get used to mind. Having mental health issues, there were plenty of times when I used to sit and do nothing but watch random programs, and half the time I was just staring at the television and could not even tell you what I had watched.

On my journey to happiness I found that doing nothing was needed for my body sometimes, but to take away the guilt of wasting time I would watch something I was interested in or that was educational. I laid down and listened to my audio books. I listen to what my body wants now and that in itself is self-care to me.

Now being a parent is a huge responsibility and one I take seriously. My view was always that I chose to have children (did not necessarily want to be a single parent though) so I was to look after them all the time. I would have family offering to take the children and I would make an excuse and politely decline.

I soon came to the conclusion that if someone you and your children know well enough offer to watch your children so you can have some time to yourself.... TAKE IT!!! I only did this when I needed them watching for a specific reason. Now I make a reason, not too often mind, but I am learning that I need to live too and they have loads of fun and treats so it's not doing them any harm.

Also it helps me clear my mind and I become a better mother for it. I don't shout as much or get annoyed as quickly. We all appreciate each other more.

It was hard the first time I did it and had no plans. My first thought was how the hell can I have someone watch them while I just sit and do nothing? Oh my, I felt so lost. The silence was killing me, I felt so alone and I did not like it one bit. The house seems so big and empty. I waited a few hours then went back for the kids early. I tried it on nights out with friends and even stayed out. I remember staying over in a hotel with my friend, we had such a good night, I laughed so much.

The next morning she thought I was insane, I got up at 8am had a shower, got ready, put in some eye drops, packed my bags and said my train is due about 9am. I did the same almost every time and would be home before lunch time to get my children. I was always conscious of the time I had left them and felt I was inconveniencing whoever had my children.

Also I did not want to abuse their help, even though I would have loved a lie in, I just couldn't. If you're a single parent you may be like me you will have forgot what a lie in feels like any way. The body clock is well and truly set to rise early regardless, or maybe it's just me?

It was not long after my relationship ended with the children's father that I decided to go on a quick holiday with my family, leaving the children with their dad. I needed to clear my head. It was a very, very, very long week.

I did enjoy myself, as I forced myself to embrace the time away from my children. I did however plan my day and night around 'Face Timing' them. (How fortunate are we now that even though we may be in another country we can still see our loved ones... it's amazing when you really think about it). It was the first time I had ever left them for more than a night. I felt awful and have not done it again since.

Anyway, self-care. It's a time to be 'selfish' but not guilty and you focus on you. I love it now. I love me. I respect me. I have self-worth. My self-care differs and can sometimes be a spur of the moment opportunity.

I love long walks on the beach, or in the country, just breathing and forgetting about all the drama in my life, and focusing instead on the beauty of the world. I don't smoke, I only occasionally drink, I don't spend a fortune on coffees which seems the latest craze, I only buy clothes when I really need them, so I allow myself to indulge on personal development with courses, books and audio books.

I have my monthly birch box subscription, go and get my hair done, have a lash lift, the occasional facial, beauty treatment and a monthly full body massage. If I don't look after me who will? If I am a worn out mess who will look after my kids? We only get one body so it's only right we do our best to look after it.

I am a qualified holistic massage therapist and I highly recommend massage, the benefits are amazing. I look at having a massage like giving my body a huge thank you and make a point of getting one as often as I can. Our body is under so much stress and tension it needs a release at some point.

That coupled with exercise helps to improve your posture also. Helping your posture enables you to breath more freely... see it's all coming together.

Your body really is your temple, so ensure you treat it with the respect it deserves. I want this body of mine to serve me for many years to come. I want to be in the best condition I can be to continue to raise my children.

Self-care has helped my mind, body and spirit, it's also benefiting my children as well as all those who I surround myself with.

Quotes

'As life goes on it becomes tiring to keep up the character you invented for yourself, and so you relapse into individuality and become more like yourself every day. This is sometimes disconcerting for those around you, but a great relief to the person concerned.'
~ Agatha Christie

'When we truly care for ourselves, it becomes possible to care far more profoundly about other people. The more alert and sensitive we are to our own needs the more loving and generous we can be towards others.'
~ Eda LeShan

'To love oneself is the beginning of a lifelong romance.'
~ Oscar Wilde

*'It's not selfish to love yourself, take care of yourself, and to make your happiness a priority.
It's necessary.'*
~ Mandy Hale

Did you know?

- ➤ Studies at the University of Michigan have found that a lack of privacy or 'me' time is a bigger cause of unhappy marriages than a less-than-satisfying sex life.

- ➤ Alone time helps reboot our brain, improves concentration and aids in problem solving.

- ➤ Research has shown that the quality of our sleep is affected by how positive or negative our thoughts are as we drift off.

- ➤ Self-care can reduce stress.

- ➤ If the average person sees a doctor 3 times a year for 10 minutes each time (total 1/2hour), the rest of the time (365 days x 24 = 8759.5 hours) is self-care.

Putting it into practice

- ❖ Schedule in some 'me time' to do something you enjoy, something just for you, or enjoy it even if you do nothing.

- ❖ Go for a walk in nature and use your senses to take in the experience.

- ❖ If you have family, wake up 30 minutes before everyone else and start your day right.

- ❖ You don't always have to be alone in me time, invite friends round for a get together just the girls or just the lads. Have games nights, quiz night, just something you will enjoy and will allow your brain to just switch of and just enjoy yourself.

- ❖ We often feel guilty for enjoying ourselves thinking there is something else we should be doing. I'm here to tell you there is a time for work and a time for living your life. We get one shot at life and we need to ensure we spend it wisely.

Download your FREE daily 'me time' guide sheet from www.attunedmindset.co.uk to ensure you start as you mean to go on.

What have you taken from this chapter?

What one thing will you implement going forward?

Notes

Chapter 5: Life begins as you step out of your comfort zone

'Life begins at the end of your comfort zone.'
~ Neale Donald Walsch

What is a comfort zone?

The definition of a comfort zone is:

A situation in which you feel comfortable and in which your ability and determination are not being tested.

It can also be seen as your 'boundaries' which you stay inside in order to stop feeling uncomfortable. If you don't push past your comfort zone you won't know what failure feels like. Richard Branson was quoted saying 'you have to be willing to fail if you are going to learn... challenges are not threats; they are opportunities'. We learn from our mistakes/failures.

The one thing that stops us stepping outside our comfort zone is fear (this will be discussed in chapter 6.) Put fear aside and think of a time you were pushed outside your comfort zone, did you feel good after? Challenging yourself is helping you to grow as a person. If we stay in the same spot nothing will change and our life will be dictated to by fear of doing something new.

Just doing a small challenge each day can help to get you moving. Say Hi to a stranger... worst outcome they ignore you (they may be having a bad day), best outcome they say Hi back.

Start to talk to someone about the weather...worst outcome they give a one word answer or none (again they may be having a bad day) best outcome you find it's a great conversation topic that everyone is aware of and it kills some awkward silence.

Ask for discount in a retail shop... worst outcome is they can only say no, then you laugh it off and say it was worth a try... best outcome you save some money, bonus!!

Going back to 1908 a study was conducted by Yerkes and Dodson. They found that when in a state of relative comfort it creates a steady level of performance. In order to maximize performance we need a state of relative anxiety, which involves increasing our stress levels slightly higher than normal.

On the flip side, too much anxiety and we become unproductive and our performance drops. So we need to find our 'Optimal Anxiety'. To find your Optimal level you need to begin to slowly step out your comfort zone and into 'optimal performance zone' (White, 2009).

It's the same with everything in life, the more you do something the easier it becomes. It's always good to see the science in a subject. The limits of possibility are endless as you expand the barriers of your comfort zone.

The key is to start small and take your time so you don't push the boundaries too far. Once you become in tune with your body you can make snap decisions, like doing things spur of the moment and you will be able trust your judgement.

Dr Brene Brown is a research professor in America and has focused her studies on courage, vulnerability, shame and empathy. I have listened to her Ted talks on The Power of Vulnerability and if you have a spare 20 minutes it's a really interesting video.

She mentions courage- which is the Latin word cor, meaning heart and definition was to speak one's mind by telling all ones heart. To put into context it is to 'tell the story of who you are with your whole heart'.

The definition of courage in the English dictionary is 'The ability to do something that frightens one; bravery'. It is with courage we can begin to step out of our comfort zone.

Through my keen interest in Brene, I found she recommended a few books and one I found interesting on title alone was by Roshi Joan Halifax who wrote a book called 'Standing at the edge: Finding freedom where fear and courage meet'.

In the book she states a number of 'edge states'- altruism, empathy, integrity, respect and engagement. She explained that each edge has a shadow, which I took as the negative side. In order to survive we need to stand on the edge to enable us to see both sides.

She explains that in life we often go over the edge but in the process we begin to learn a lot and it's not an 'end state'. She found that by going over the edge she was able to take from it compassion. As I heard Joan talk about the book as above, I realised that is what has happened to me.

Pushing myself out of my comfort zone into situations I would normally shy away from has opened my eyes to other possibilities, and I have gained much more empathy and compassion and understanding about others and more so myself.

In order to grow as individuals we need to break past the barriers we put up in what we feel is a way of protecting ourselves from hurt and pain. I hear so often the term 'barriers' 'wall' 'bubble'- where did this all come from? Well they are not real in terms of they are not physical, they are just in our mind. There is a psychological theory of repression which is in a way an unresolved inner conflict. Good old Freud made a point of repression but, as with most of psychology, over time this view has been challenged.

It actual goes back a long time even before Freud although the understanding was not the same as it is today, yet is interlinked with other psychological phenomena if you wish to delve deeper.

One of the causes I found while searching for answers was 'resistance is fear'. We don't like to feel fearful therefore we avoid situations which may cause us fear. So in order to step out of the comfort zone we need to tackle our fear (can you see how they all intertwine now?).

Therefore the barriers, walls, bubbles we encapsulate ourselves in is of our own doing. When we fall into situations out of our control, and feel bad, negative emotions, we never want to be in the same position again, I mean why would we want to relive those moments?

Well the truth is there will always be testing times in life and we cannot completely avoid bad or negative situations which in turn lead to bad and/or negative emotions. We then condition ourselves to become more resilient. What we have to do is become aware of the situations and emotions and learn to deal with them more effectively and stop living in fear. I will leave this here as the next topic is Fear!

My experience

My comfort zone now compared to a few years ago is completely different. Before my self-discovery journey my comfort zone was my protective bubble and leaving it was never an option. It's a reason I never got over my social anxiety quicker. I was never one for making myself uncomfortable on purpose.

Skip to now and I love the thrill of stepping outside it and seeing what is truly possible. I challenge myself daily to do at least one thing that makes me feel uncomfortable but that I know will be rewarding after. I came across a lady called Mel Robbins and her concept of the 5 second rule (not the one where food hits the floor and it's safe to eat if you retrieve it within 5 seconds …bork).

I use this now for almost everything, and don't over think it. Like getting up when I really, really, really don't want to. I only second guess if I feel there is an element of risk to my life. I am sure you can tell I love my life, so I am not about to be reckless with it.

I say this due to a liberating incident where I went on holiday following the break up and we went to a cliff where people were jumping off. We only went for the scenery but anyway I had a little voice in my head saying 'go, be free and jump'. With wobbly legs (should have known then) I went to the top trying to help my nephew to jump. Then I got closer to the edge and well FEAR washed all over me.

There was a guy there who gave me all the encouragement and safety talk I needed and I then said right after 3, about 10 times, then just said 'Right I'm doing it' 1, 2, jump.... Wow the free fall took forever, so long that I panicked and decided to adopt a sitting position... yeah you guessed it... I landed on my butt... awwwwwww... as I went under the water I heard a big almighty 'ooooooooo' from the 20-30 spectators.

I remember thinking I am going really far down here, oh I guess I better kick my legs and get to the top. At that point I let out an almighty 'F%&* THAT HURT'.

As I got to the side and stepped out of the water another 'ooooo' came from the crowd, my butt was a lovely shade of black, blue and red. I was not big and not clever and I don't recommend that anyone does this to get out their comfort zone on a whim, with 'no diving or jumping from a height in to water' experience.

So lesson learned, assess the risk and your 'actual' ability first. Don't be foolish like me.

It has taken me a while to be able to see the benefits of stepping out of this so called comfort zone. I had the disillusion it was there as a protector, my safety zone as you will.

As someone who was not a people person, I find that my social comfort zone was nonexistent but as I have forced myself to step outside it so many times recently and I now love it. I push myself into new situations, I am not afraid to attend events on my own.

I will admit the nerves always follow me but they make me feel alive and I always come out of it having met amazing new people.

I remember going to an event at university as I had been nominated for an award and, well, I wanted to see if I had a shot of winning. There were so many people and I only knew a handful to say hello to and that was about it.

As I approached the building for the event I heard a little voice in my head saying... 'What the hell are you doing?!?!?' I kept walking thinking I am not sure but I am doing it anyway. I walked in and felt like a lost puppy.

I saw someone I recognized, introduced myself, gave the old 'I'm on my own can I tag along with you please' and latched on to mamma June, who is amazing. We sat at a table of new faces and I felt awkward, however, I smiled said Hi and then clammed up, still smiling.

Then all their friends came and I and mama June had to move tables. So we moved to a table full of gentlemen, where we exchanged awkward hellos after interrupting their table mid chat.

While taking in the atmosphere June talked to all the people she knew. I overheard the guys on my table chatting about mental health... ping... my kind of conversation, without thinking I was already out of my comfort zone and chatting away to these guys whom I am now friends with.

It was a stroke of luck I met them because there was another award night not long after and I was back in the lost puppy mode. I actually ended up tagging along with them for the rest of the night and off into the town after.

Normally I would of shied away negatively talking myself out of the situation, thinking I would not fit in or that what I had to say would not be relevant. The people I have met through university are more welcoming than I could have ever hoped and it's such a community vibe.

I look back and imagine what it would have been like if I never spoke and let my fear of leaving my comfort zone take over. I tend to think what's the worst that can happen? They don't like me, and that's ok not everyone has to like everyone, hey I may not even like them. Some people just don't 'vibe' as I like to call it but when you meet people you do 'vibe' with, it's immense.

Another way I now like to go out my comfort zone is public speaking. It's as daunting as meeting new people but again it's make or break as they say. As long as I know what I am saying I pretend that people want to listen.

University has been a game changer for me, I found a whole new level of confidence. In my first year I addressed the whole of my cohort without even thinking. I love to do it now. I always used to go bright red and limit what I had to say so I could deflect the limelight. Now I enjoy the limelight to a certain degree, but when I share my passion and enthusiasm I feel I have found my calling in life.

Once I began to understand the term 'Comfort zone' and what it entailed it was like a lightbulb moment. I began to think back about all the times that could be seen as me stepping outside my level of comfort.

As I noted them down I realised just how far I had come in life and if I had not done those things which challenged me to step out from my normal realm of comfort I would not be the woman I am today. I would not have learnt so many lessons, I would not have felt a whole range of emotions, and I would not have experienced life.

I also realised that a lot of the times when I breached the zone of safety which I also see it as, it was out of my control. Like being asked to do something for someone who I did not want to let down or something as simple as having children and needing to take them to school which meant potentially talking to parents.

Oh and all the parties your child gets invited to which you don't want them to miss out. Most of the time you stay with your child and this means either sitting silently avoiding contact (the old me loved this) or starting a conversation (the new me- on occasions).

I also realised that my mental health plays a big part in whether I have the ability to step outside my comfort zone. My mind has a way of playing nasty tricks on me and convincing me to retreat and stay in my 'bubble', but now I have self-awareness I can fight off the little voice in my head and, (without sounding like I have lost the plot), internally laugh at the negative voice as I know I am about to prove it wrong and throw myself in to situations that I happen to get myself into by having a productive day and act like a social butterfly, only to sit back and remember I have social anxiety.

It's a never ending battle for me and my crazy ass mind. However, what I can say is I am in control now. I remind myself of the times I overcome situations and the feeling of adrenaline and achievement, I get an overwhelming sense of pride.

I also think that is why I procrastinate over stepping outside the comfort zone- will it have been a waste of my precious time? Would I look back and say 'Why did I waste time worrying, it was fine!' If the answer is yes to wasting time I just get on with it, or if the answer is no then I know I need a little more time to think about what it is I am about to do, but not too much time of course or it totally defeats the objective. I hope that makes some sort of sense☺.

Overall, I now challenge myself to push the limits of my comfort zone and take something away from it on how I felt, how I can improve, just something positive to encourage me to keep doing it!

Quotes

'When you go out of your comfort zone and it works. There's nothing more satisfying.'
~ Kristen Wiig

'Unless you try to do something beyond what you have already mastered, you will never grow.'
~Ralph Woldo Emerson

'Luck is what happens when preparation meets opportunity.'
~ Seneca

'Don't be afraid to take an unfamiliar path. Sometimes they are the ones that take you to the best places.'
~Unknown

Did you know?

- History has repeatedly told us that if we never go beyond our comfort zone we will never learn.

- Henry Ford- founder of the Ford Motor Group. He failed and went broke five times before he finally succeeded.

- Walt Disney- he needs no introduction! He was fired for lacking imagination and had no good ideas. He was declared bankrupt several times before he finally built Disney.

- Dr. Seuss' first book was rejected by 27 publishers, the 28th sold 6 million copies.

- Each of these successful individuals went beyond what others would see as limitations. They stepped outside their comfort zone despite on occasions it not being the best place to be but they kept going knowing something better was on the other side if they keep pursuing.

Putting it into practice

- ❖ Do something small every day to push yourself out of your comfort zone.

- ❖ Think of sometimes when you have pushed past your comfort zone and what you felt before and after. Then use that when taking out your small challenges.

- ❖ Once you have pushed past a comfort zone write it down and acknowledge how far you have come. Reward yourself and be proud.

- ❖ If you don't want to do it alone then find an accountable buddy who will do it with you or be there for support and encouragement.

Visit www.attunedmindset.co.uk to find ways to break out of your comfort zone to ensure you start as you mean to go on.

What have you taken from this chapter?

....
....
....
....
....
....
....
....
....
....
....
....
....
....
....
....
....
....
....
....
....
....
....
....
....

What one thing will you implement going forward?

Notes

Chapter 6: Use your fear to soar

'Feel the fear and do it anyway.'
~ Susan Jefferes

What are fears and limitations?

Fear has a few definitions:

1. An unpleasant emotion caused by the threat of danger, pain, or harm.

2. A feeling of anxiety concerning the outcome of something or the safety of someone.

3. The likelihood of something unwelcome happening.

4. A mixed feeling of dread and reverence.

Fear is a chain reaction in the brain that starts with a stressful stimulus and ends with the release of chemicals that cause a racing heart, fast breathing and energised muscles, among other things, also known as the fight-or-flight response.

The fear response is almost entirely autonomic, meaning the process is almost entirely unconscious. Have you heard a loud band and jumped 'out of your skin'? You never planned to, your body did it as a response to what it feels is a threat.

Fight or flight was first termed by an American psychologist and Professor Walter Bradford Cannon in 1932. The brain senses a threat, our body releases hormones then our body reacts accordingly. It actually goes all the way back to our evolutionary existence when we would have to rapidly respond to threats in order to survive in the wild.

A range of studies conducted around the subject 'perceived control,' and it has been proven that it is an important construct to physical and psychological wellbeing. Perceived control refers to an individual's belief about their own capability. Through therapy it is possible to modify levels of fear by taking a different perspective on the situation. Mindfulness is key to success (Pagnini and Langer, 2016).

So if we allow fear to stop us in our tracks it then sets us up with limitations on what we can and cannot do. With limitations we either set the bar too low or we aim too high. Yet we have the freedom to do anything we want to if we choose. So why is it we limit our lives? Usually it is because we are concerned about what others think of us. We give up on our dreams because of fear of failure. It all connects.

When it comes to motivational speeches Winston Churchill is a man I admire in terms of his commitment and passion in his words. When he spoke, people listened. One quote which has been influential in my journey is: 'Success consists of going from failure to failure without loss of enthusiasm.

One big fear is that of failure, no one wants to fail! He also said 'If you're going through hell, keep going.' Not only was Churchill inspirational but without realising it he coined the term 'the black dog' to describe his depression.

He also struggled with suicidal thoughts. He used paining as his release of emotions. In an interview he asked the gentleman interviewing if he was a worrier, to which came the answer 'yes'.

Churchill replied 'The recognising and acknowledging of fear is a mark of wisdom.'. The World Health Organization released an animation which I feel explains what it's like to have depression in terms of the 'black dog'. (Find the links on my website: www.attunedmindset.co.uk)

Another influential person for me is Will

Smith, his motivational videos around fear are inspiring. The fact he is now on Instagram I love to follow him and his motivational posts. He describes fear as jumping out of a plane and once you get past the point of fear its bliss. Why do we work ourselves up to be fearful prior to the actual event which then ruins everything?

'God placed the best things in life on the other side of terror, on the other side of your maximum fear are all of the best things in life.' Once you pass your fear doesn't it feel good, amazing even. Do you then think, why did I work myself up so much? What a waste of your emotions and time which could have been spent on something else.

Fear can last for a short amount of time and pass. Other times it can stay with us much longer. In some cases it may stay with us all our lives and take over. If can affect our appetite, sleep, concentration and of course our mental health. Once hormones are released they send a signal to the brain.

A part called the amygdala which helps us to focus on emotions, survival instincts and memory. Link fear to a negative emotion and that's how the memory will be stored, the brain remembers all details such as sound, sights, smells and the next time we are presented with the same sound, sight or smells it recalls the memory of fear.

There have been many articles I have read

which state we need to use fear. When fear rises we should recognise it and not deny it. We should focus on what we need to do to keep the fear from turning into panic.

So we all know that fear exists but now we know we have the choice to either live in fear, or we can learn to overcome and work with fear and live despite it.

My experience

Fear is a big issue for me and it's all down to a lot of years giving myself negative self-talk. I was an over thinker to the extreme. I listened to what a few people said and deemed that to be true. I was a quitter, I did not know what I wanted in life, I gave up when the going got tough, I doubted myself, I set my limits too low, I never allowed myself to be better.

Fear can ruin your life. I let it ruin mine for far too long. I wish I knew then what I know now, hence writing this book to hopefully get someone off the fear train sooner rather than later. Fear is an emotion created from a perception which most of the time is made up in our head.

I have always been a dreamer, I don't know why but I always let other people's fears stop my dreams becoming a reality. Have you ever told someone your plans and they try to talk you out of it by telling you all the reasons it won't work?

They would plant seeds of doubt that would become weeds and kill my seeds before they had time to bloom. I would always want success more than anything but in the back of my mind there was always self-doubt. I would have all the right intentions going into new projects and then the minute something didn't work I would back down.

It's not that I was afraid of the hard work,

looking back I was afraid of the failure so I succumb to it before it got too hard.

I remember a certain turning point and it's where I have always grown from in terms of where I want to be in life.

It was when I met my amazing Prince's Trust mentor Dave. He is a very wise man and whom I owe a lot of my success, drive and determination to.

At the time I applied for the prince's trust I was trying to make a living as a single mum of two. It felt like a final push to make something of myself. I was 29 so just within the age bracket to apply (everything happens for a reason).

I met with Dave and he has been my guru if you like ever since. Dave has seen me go through leaving my apprenticeship to going solo in a gym and starting my massage business.

The gym never worked out as it was not the environment for me. Also going through the split at the time was having massive effects on my mental health. I then decided to leave the gym and found a hairdresser who had space for me to do my business.

This was a new salon and I had to work hard to get clients for my business. Suddenly the owner shut shop and I was lost again. Knowing I had children and bills to sort I got myself a job in a call center part time for a steady income and then worked mobile when I could.

I felt like I was finally getting somewhere. I was overcoming all the hurdles and put my fears of failing away as I was determined to make a decent life for me and my children.

Suddenly a little over a week before my 30th birthday I was admitted to a stoke ward in a local hospital. Thankfully it was not a stoke, it was determined that I had suffered with functional neurological symptoms which did not fit under any specific diagnosis.

Now this is what I would class as fear! I knew at that point I had to take note of what my body was telling me. I was not even 30 yet and I was the youngest person on a stroke ward for 3 days. I knew I had to actually face up to some of the issues I was facing and stop avoiding them.

The main things being the ongoing battle with my children's father and the whole situation surrounding it. It again got me back to gratitude and my mindset. I went to the Dr. and asked for help in terms of talking therapy and set about having CBT (Cognitive Behavioral Therapy) this worked a dream for changing my way of thinking and gave me new tools to cope with the situations in my life.

It got me thinking too about the situation instead of blocking it out. It was the beginning of my ideas for this book and my future. I realized I was being drawn to speaking out about mental wellbeing. I wanted to educate others and encourage them to take control of the mental wellbeing, just like I have, and to highlight the amazing services and tools available.

Again my mentor said words to me that just stuck- 'only you can control your thoughts'. This made me realize that only I can change my way of thinking, why did I want to damage myself by thinking so negative and critical all the time.

It also made me realize I was a massive control freak and a big fear was letting go of that control. Having said that, now I realized I was the only one who could control my thoughts I also realized that meant I could not control how other people thought. This was a huge revelation, I was also a massive over thinker, not so much now. I would think of all the worst scenarios and play them out in my head.

My worst scenarios I literally mean played out all my fears and did so over and over again. With the combination of my therapist, my mentor and the information I was collecting around mindset I was making progress.

Within a short few weeks I had gone from one end of the scale to the other and was advised I was no longer in need of sessions. Then a new fear hit, how will I cope without these session.

It's something I want to work on in terms of where to go after the therapy stops and you're on your own again, just you and your thoughts.

I again went looking for another audio to keep expanding my mindset and came across 'The answer, by Allan and Barbara Pease'. Audio is the best when the authors are reading it, it had me laughing at parts, they are comics and I wonder if they know it?

Their audio flicked on so many light bulbs in my head and I found a lot of what I had been learning coming together. I found my fears were slowly leaving me and replaced with a sheer determination to get the life I dreamed so hard about.

I quit my secure job in the call center shortly after my hospital stay and I got myself an ideal job with the council, due to very long delays in the process I gave up hope of it ever becoming a reality so took another bold move and enrolled as a full time student at University.

Not only did I enroll and gain a place, the university I choose was only an hour away from my home.

Did everyone support me? Nope! You may have guessed that people put their fears on me and tried to point out the limitations. I understood based on my past impulsive actions and lack of following through.

They just did not have faith in my new found power like I did. It's the strangest empowering feeling and one I wish everyone could feel. I made strict plans and it was as if a fairy had waved her magic wand, (minus the glitter dust ☹) everything fell into place.

It has to be the best decision I have ever made. Has it been easy? No. Has it been worth it? Yes. I faced my fears over and over again and did it anyway, ignoring others' fears along the way. It was so satisfying to finish my first year and say 'and you all thought it was never going to work'. I never quit, even when it gets tough.

I work harder than I have ever done before and I kept on believing in myself and my dreams. I do it because I have undeniable faith that I can. I use all that I have learnt and put it into practice. I am now turning my dreams into reality even if they change along the way, I am proud of myself and the person I have become despite any fears or limitations.

Quotes

'There would be nothing to frighten you if you refused to be afraid.'
~Mahatma Ghandi

'Being brave isn't the absence of fear. Being brave is having that fear but finding a way through it.'
~Bear Grylls

'I learned that courage was not the absence of fear, but the triumph over it. The brave man is not he who does not feel afraid, but he who conquers that fear.'
~ Nelson Mandela

'Fear is not real. It is a product of thought you create. Do not misunderstand me. Danger is very real. But fear is a choice.'
~ Will Smith

Did you know?

- Fear is healthy! Lack of fear has been shown to be a sign of serious brain damage. It's a normal part of a functioning brain.

- You don't need to see fear to trigger a reaction, the thought alone causes a reaction. Over thinking can create imaginary fear which could turn into chronic anxiety and become debilitating.

- Most fear is learnt- fear comes with knowledge and experience.

- You should FACE YOUR FEAR- (in a controlled and safe environment depending on the fear) avoiding fear makes it worse.

Putting it into practice

- ❖ What stops you from achieving what you really want? When you find the answer you can begin on finding a solution.

- ❖ Set small goals, write them down, then write your actions on how you can achieve them, then give yourself a reasonable time limit, then write how you will feel when you accomplish this and really get attached to the feelings, finally write down how you will reward yourself (it does not have to cost a fortune but just a little something to mark your achievement.)

Visit www.attunedmindset.co.uk to see more tools on goal setting and overcoming fears and limitations to ensure you start as you mean to go on.

What have you taken from this chapter?

What one thing will you implement going forward?

....
....
....
....
....
....
....
....
....
....
....
....
....
....
....
....
....
....
....
....
....
....

Notes

Chapter 7: Exercise the smart way

'A year from now, you may wish you had started today.'
~ Karen Lamb

What is exercise?

You may be thinking 'Abigail, I know what exercise is!' Let's pretend some people don't, so here is a definition:

1. Activity requiring physical effort, carried out to sustain or improve health and fitness.

2. An activity carried out for a specific purpose.

Some HATE it, some LOVE it, some are OBSESSED with it and others just don't care.

My view is that exercise is anything that gets your heart rate to change, in turn keeping it active and healthy. My main advice is to listen to your body and your mind. Make sure you do something you enjoy as that way you will put more effort in and go for longer without realizing it, resulting in you wanting to do it again and again.

Your body is an amazing object and should be treated with the respect it deserves. You only get one shot at life, remember that. I hear the phrase 'My body is my temple'- it's so true. Why we choose to punish our body by not looking after it is beyond me.

Therefore, we need to learn to change our view on how we treat our body. Exercise is one way we can look after our body and this means changing our mindset around the subject to become more positive and motivated.

As someone who likes to learn about subjects, I thought I would share some of my learnt wisdom. Let's begin with the basics of why we should exercise.

According to the World Health Organization, health is a state of complete physical, mental and social wellbeing: not merely the absence of disease or infirmity (WHO, 1946).

Regular physical activity is one of the most important things that you can do for your health. The British Heart Foundation stated in a 2017 report:
- Around 20 MILLION adults in the UK are psychically inactive.

Physical inactivity is an independent risk factor for chronic disease and is estimated to cause 5 million deaths worldwide. So, keeping our heart healthy is key. I don't know about you, but I want to live as long as I can!

The body itself, the structure, is so advanced if you choose to look into it in depth, which I did. For example, it is estimated that there are up to 650 skeletal muscles in the human body, making up about 30-50% of our body weight.

They are split into three types of muscle: Involuntary (move unconsciously- respiration), Voluntary (require conscious control- biceps) and Cardiac (heart). Muscles have four main functions: producing movement, stabilizing the body, storing and moving substances (heart pumps blood around the body) and generating heat.

With that being said, looking after our muscles is a vital part to ensure we can do all of the above. I came across the term muscle memory and heard that the key to building good muscle memory is to focus on the quality of the quantity.

After you repeatedly do something, it then becomes easier to do without thinking, so to speak. For example, riding a bike. You learn which muscles you need to engage to keep your balance, then after you have done it numerous times, you just get on with it and don't think about it.

You just do it. If we leave the muscles inactive and don't train them regularly then they lose their strength and subsequently they are not able to support your skeleton (your frame), the knock on effects begin and the longer you leave it the more the effects have a chance of becoming irreversible, such as spinal posture changes (Kyphosis-hunchback).

The term 'Fitness' refers to the ability to meet the demands of life safely and effectively, without exhaustion or undue stress. I am sure you will have seen on the news or maybe even know of someone you would deem fit but sadly, they pass away. It was always something that puzzled me until I read what fitness actually is.

Some people don't listen to their body enough and push it to its limits where it struggles to cope, resulting in injury or more tragically, death (I am not saying this relates to all incidences at all, as I don't have all the facts.

Even if I did I am not a medical professional). It is not just exercise alone that contributes, it is a variety of things such as medical issues (diagnosed or often undiagnosed), emotional and mental wellbeing, nutrition, social and environmental. So, finding a happy healthy level of exercise is important but please do so safely and if in doubt seek medical/expert advice.

Find your balance and don't be ashamed if

you struggle. Everyone starts off as a beginner. Shame on the person judging you, never shame on you. At least your making an effort to make the change.

So, we have discussed the body and touched on other factors, one being emotional and mental wellbeing. This, I find, is where people often go wrong and I will admit it was my biggest issue when it came to fitness.

There are certain barriers to fitness and exercise and they are normally based in our mind. I love the phrase 'Mind over matter' however, I love 'If I don't mind, it doesn't matter' better. The definition of a barrier is: a fence or other obstacle that prevents movement of access.

Some common barriers include:
- Anxiety and fear of feeling out of your 'comfort zone'
- Family and work commitments- lack of time
- Lack of support from friends and family
- Lack of enjoyment, motivation or energy
- Age, injury, ill health and disability
- The cost
- The weather

I am sure you may be able to add more of your own to the list. Basically, they are all excuses as there is always some way of being able to overcome them. For example:
- Work on your mindset

- Schedule time for a fun activity, wake up earlier. You only need 20-30 minutes, even if its broken up throughout the day.
- Find an online supportive community, make new likeminded friends
- Find something you enjoy such as a dance fitness class or martial arts
- Find something age appropriate, ask a medical professional what is available for you to do.
- Exercise does not need to cost! - walk/run around the block, the park, the beach. It's all free!
- It's refreshing to be out in all weathers and it adds variety. If you're in the UK, surely you're used to the unpredictable weather ☺

At the end of the day, the choice is yours on what you do but hopefully this has inspired you to take action.

My experience

As a child, I remember I used to run around a lot playing, especially on the little strip of grass (the cut) up from my house and playing Kerby (in case you're wondering what it is- with a hard football two people stand on opposite sides of the road.

The aim is to bounce the ball off the kerb to score points. If you catch the ball from the bounce, then you step in the middle *when safe to do so* and aim at the kerb to get more points unless the other person gets the ball. If they hit you with the ball before getting back to your side, they steal your points. It was the most fun game of my childhood until my street became a busy bus route).

In secondary school however, when sport became mandatory, I realized I was not athletic and did not really enjoy sport but I went along with it either to fit in or because I had no choice. It was picked up that I had issues with exercise.

The fact was, and I never told anyone of course, that when I exercised I became fearful of the feeling of my heart rate increasing, then I panicked, then I stopped, then I made it worse than it was by not breathing and on a few occasions ended up being carried back to the gym block by my teacher (who, dare I say it, was 'well fit').

It was so embarrassing. I even used to pretend

to go over on my ankle to get out of it or find any reason to not join in when it was something that would get my heart racing. I even forgot my PE kit. Big mistake, as I then had to get the spare kits from the dreaded, stinking, sweaty box, and it was vile.

My favorite was the javelin, although the girl I always competed against put my throws to utter shame. I loved netball. I even joined a local league with my one friend and I had no clue about the rules. I went to try and fit in but this never happened, *shock*. I went to represent the school at various events in athletics and was regularly on the relay team (200m on the bend). Anyway, a visit to the Doctor after my PE teacher became concerned resulted in me being told that all I needed was a banana before exercise- who knew!

After leaving school, I found I did nothing fitness related apart from the odd DVD at home when I felt a tad motivated, but the same old script bored me and it went in the DVD cupboard never to been seen again, *until I moved out.*

I joined a few gyms and only went to the classes but I would get bored. Then, one night, I fell asleep on the sofa at my parents' and woke up to the adverts which were showing a new fitness craze called Zumba. You could buy the whole set of DVDs for a special price!

I thought, wow, I love the music, I love to dance. *It always looks better in my mind than the reality.* I thought I could do this, so I ordered the box of DVDs. After using them and loving them, I found out I could become an instructor! I joined a local class and shortly after I was on the stage as an extra alongside the instructor for my impressive moves!

This spurred me on to become an instructor and out of concern, I was not qualified to teach fitness. I went on a course to become a qualified Exercise to Music instructor and I began to teach the classes myself! Who knew being on stage on my own with 20+ people relying on me to get their exercise fix would be something I could do. It was never planned, it just happened. I guess I was being an actress and 'performing'.

Then, I became pregnant shortly after and stopped teaching, which was a personal choice. I eventually went back to teaching but as a cover instructor for some friends and a local gym. Then, life took over and I moved to a new town and stopped teaching altogether.

I then had my little fella and decided that I really wanted to get into shape, so joined a gym and got myself a personal trainer. I loved the gym, I loved lifting weights and seeing my body change. I began working in the gym as a massage therapist and class instructor.

I worked hard to get my level 2 Gym and level 3 personal trainer certificate. I did not want to be a PT, I just wanted the knowledge. I went to a few different PTs to see what style worked best for myself. That's when I met my favorite PT called Lee, who taught me about functional training. Sadly, I was battling heavily through my mental health issues at this point so I was constantly moaning and finding excuses.

I never fully committed to completing each program as my negative self-talk would always take over, also finances had took a hit so I stopped training. This became a cycle for me of trying to get back on track then falling back and losing interest. I could never understand why but now I do. My mind was all over the place.

As I mentioned in Chapter 3, I began to run and I slowly built up using the Army's fitness app for the fitness side, as well as the running. I stuck on an audio book and turned on the motivation prompts from the app and I was off.

Not far, but it was huge for me who always flaked out at school. I often went back to exercise hard in the past for all of the wrong reasons. I would do it out of frustration and generally cause some kind of injury in the process, meaning I was back to not exercising.

I now understand my body and listen to it completely. I take my time to enable myself to stay in the game. I do what makes me feel good and I am not hard on myself. I enjoy hiking, walks on the beach, weight training, body resistance and interval running.

I always try to be outside and change my surroundings to stop myself becoming bored. I love listening to different audio, as I struggle to sit and read, so it saves me time, too. Not to mention I forget I'm exercising and do it longer. I can learn and get fit at the same time- bonus. Some days, I have to force myself. Having my stuff ready the night before helps.

I also do it first thing to ensure it's done, as the further through a busy day, the less likely I am to do anything due to tiredness. Basically, if there is a will there is a way. As with everything in this book, it's all down to you. Only you can choose to make the change but you also have to want the change. It's about connecting with your reason why. Set SMART goals. Keep it small, realistic and achievable to keep you motivated.

I quickly realized I needed to set smaller goals as I am the kind of person who wants to see immediate results. The minute I realized there is no such thing as a quick fix was the minute I knew I had to work on my mindset more. I had to find a way to keep me motivated while I waited for the results.

Taking photos for my own personal use was a great indicator. I began to look in the mirror more and appreciate the body I had with all the curves and really studied my body. The only difference is that I studied it with love. I knew that anything I was not particularly happy with could be worked on with some effort.

How could I hate my body when I was not doing anything to change it? It was all in my mind. I had to want to change, I had to put in some effort if I wanted to make changes.

It is a long process, I won't lie, but one thing I am more aware of and changing my mindset has helped me so much. Learning about health and fitness has been a big key to changing my mindset. I educate myself to know more and it's the inspiration I needed to make changes and to keep myself on track. Sometimes knowing the hard facts can help motivate you. Having children, I need to be the role model they deserve and teach them the right things. There is no point preaching to them and not doing anything myself.

I do what makes me happy and never put pressure on myself. Nine times out of 10, I actually surprise myself with how much I can achieve. Mind over matter!

Quotes

'Exercise is king. Nutrition is queen. Put them together and you've got a kingdom.'
~ Jack Lalanne

'My toughest opponent has always been me.'
~Muhammad Ali

'No matter how old you are, you can exercise and feel good.'
~ Jo Wicks

'If you're tired of starting over, stop giving up.'
~Shia Labeouf

Did you know?

> ➢ *Guidelines: to stay healthy, adults aged 19-64 should try to be active daily and should do at least 150 minutes of moderate aerobic activity, such as cycling or brisk walking every week and strength exercises on 2 or more days a week that work all the major muscles (legs, hips, back, abdomen, chest, shoulders and arms).*

> ➢ It can reduce your risk of major illnesses, such as heart disease, type 2 diabetes by up to 50%.

> ➢ Lowers risk of early death by up to 30%.

> ➢ Research has shown that physical activity can boost self-esteem, mood, sleep quality and energy as well as reducing the risk of stress, depression, dementia and Alzheimer's.

> ➢ Muscles work in pairs.

> ➢ Regular physical activity reduces the risk of coronary heart disease by up to 35%.

> ➢ From the age of 40, our muscular system starts its decline, leading to loss

of muscle mass which in turn leads to reduction in power, strength and endurance. This can then go on to reductions in support of the skeleton and weakness in motor skills, especially balance and co-ordination.

Putting it into practice

- ❖ Find a small pocket of time to do something fun. As long as you're moving you're working out.

- ❖ Start small and build up.

- ❖ Listen to your body.

- ❖ I believe you should also listen to your body (not your head, or you will end up talking yourself out of it.) Your mind will give up before your body does if you give it the chance. Have you ever worked out and felt like quitting but pushed on for one more or ran a little further? That's because your body will go on longer than your mind. So, take your mind off what you're doing and you will last longer. Listen to music/audio or chat with friends.

Visit www.attunedmindset.co.uk to find hints and tips to help with your fitness goals and ensure you start as you mean to go on.

What have you taken from this chapter?

....
....
....
....
....
....
....
....
....
....
....
....
....
....
....
....
....
....
....
....
....
....

What one thing will you implement going forward?

Notes

Chapter 8: Fuel your body to happiness

'Every time you eat or drink you are either... feeding disease or fighting it.'
~ Heather Morgan

What is Nutrition?

The World Health Organizations defines nutrition as follows:
Nutrition is the intake of food, considered in relation to the body's dietary needs. Good nutrition – an adequate, well balanced diet combined with regular physical activity – is a cornerstone of good health.

Poor nutrition can lead to reduced immunity, increased susceptibility to disease, impaired physical and mental development, and reduced productivity.

Basically, nutrition is feeding your body, mind and soul. The process of providing or obtaining the food necessary for health and growth.
Diet is influenced by many factors such as income, culture, social and economic, to name a few. It is also down to individual preference.

There are so many different guidelines and so many people/celebrities and companies trying to influence the world. It's overwhelming and also confusing. The issue presented is that each person has their own body type and their own requirements so there can never be a one diet that fits all.

It's all about educating yourself on what works best for you, not your best friend of someone you follow on social media, but you.

Times are changing and packaging is becoming a little more clear as to what is inside but at the end of the day, businesses want to make money and advertising sells.

They play to the audience who want to be healthy but don't know the full facts. Low-fat- Must contain less than 3g of fat per 100g of food. (Watch out for added sugar as a compromise.) No Added Sugar-Must have no sugar or sweetener added. (This does not means low in sugar or sugar free, as some products contain natural sugars.)

I chose to educate myself after seeing and hearing so much from those around me and information on the internet/magazines. We should all take the time to learn about how to fuel our body effectively and responsibly.

Our body is clever.

Think of this, more research is showing we are what we eat... So, why would we want to fill it with junk food? Our digestive system works by taking the nutrients and excreting waste products. As a rule of thumb, if you can't pronounce the ingredients then it's not healthy. It's a substance-made product.

What's wrong with going back to nature? One of the issues we face now is the soil depleting due to erosion and pollution according to WWF, who warned that actions needs to be taken to avoid jeopardizing future food production and provision of clean water.

Therefore, there is potential for a decline in nutritional content of fruit and vegetables. As a result, foods are being genetically modified and using pesticides. How about we grown our own? Become self-sufficient? It's an option. At least you know the full background on your food.

According to www.express.co.uk in an article from 2016 on vitamin use, 'Britons splash £400 million on vitamins every year to stay healthy.' Research estimated that it would rise 2% in 2017. We are turning to supplements in order to gain the added nutrition we need.

There are minimum guidelines to follow but they are just that minimum guideline, and again, based on the individual you may need to increase. It's best to seek advice from a health professional to ensure you're getting the correct advice. Articles and publications that are free are often generic, so ensure whatever choice you make works for you and your body alone.

While doing my fitness training, we touched on nutrition. I was intrigued by the Health Belief Model developed in the 1950's by social psychologists Hochbaum, Rosenstock and Kegels who worked for the U.S Public Health Service.

Its focus is on the attitudes and beliefs of individuals. It is based on the understanding that an individual will take action if an adverse health condition can be avoided, however, as with most models, it has its limitations, one of which is it does not take into account other factors which may influence health behaviors. So, our health depends on our approach in terms of what we think and believe.

On further investigation, I came across the Health Locus of Control scales, which was developed by Julian Rotter in 1954. The concept is used in personality psychology, but can be applied to educational, health and clinical psychology.

The main belief is that individuals have

control over their own situation and can affect it in a positive or negative manner.

	Perceived locus of control	
	Internal	**External**
Attributions of no control	Ability	Change/Luck
Attributions of control	Effort	Task Difficulty

So, basically, people with internal locus of control believe that the outcomes of their actions are a result of their own abilities, whereas people with external locus of control blame others or external circumstances. Which one are you?

The theory that interested me and helped change my thought process was Self-Efficiency. This is the belief of a person on whether or not they think they can be successful at achieving an action. It plays a massive part in whether or not we can achieve a goal.

It is developed from external experiences. Having a high level of self-efficiency will change the way you look at a challenge in that you will be more likely to see it as something to master rather than something to avoid. Low self-efficiency results in avoiding the challenge at all cost.

So, how can we increase our levels? Well, in 1992, Rald Schwarzer developed the Health

Action Process Approach. It's a theoretical framework to explain, predict and modify health behaviors. It's based on goal setting and goal pursuit, targeting the motivation phase or the violation phase. In my words, it is finding what motivates you and working on that or identifying what is getting in the way of your progress and overcoming it.

There will always be factors affecting participation in activity, such as demographics, culture, physical challenges, current skills and so on. I have only mentioned a few theories yet there are many more around our behavior and why we do what we do.

It's the reason I chose to study Psychology. We are fascinating creatures and I want to understand more. It is up to us as individuals to take control, and instead of making excuses we need to be asking ourselves how we can overcome them and essentially flip them from a negative to a positive. We are the only barrier to our own success. Let's find ways to lift the barriers.

My experience

Love, hate and hate some more. As a female, I have always had body insecurities. Why? I honestly have no idea if I am being completely honest. I feel a lot of it has come from subconsciously taking in what is around me and what others are saying.

Through my childhood, I was always a good eater in terms of not being that fussy. I didn't think about what I was eating or what others thought.

When it came to secondary school, I believe that was when things started to change. I was able to pick anything from the school lunch. I had money but followed the trend of chips and gravy most days, then leaving school grounds to go to the local shop for a sandwich and, of course, crisps, chocolate, fizzy drinks and sweets.

I suppose because I was always someone who followed the crowd to fit in, I picked up the habits of those around me. I remember at one point I became really concerned with my body and I hated it. As I mentioned in Chapter 4, I would cry in the shower, grabbing my skin and wanting so badly to rip it off.

The thought even crossed my mind to cut it off but I knew that was not an option. I instead decided to eat very little. I would lie about what I had eaten and became really down. At school, I remember sitting in class and not feeling too well (lack of food) when a friend at the time told the teachers she had noticed I was not eating and had concerns.

There had begun my first experience of counselling and the label 'Eating Disorder' on my medical record. I hated counselling so badly and refused to go back after two sessions. It simply made me feel worse. In my view, the whole situation was dealt with so badly that I ended up faking my way out of it to get everyone off my back.
I would not say I yo-yo dieted because I never stuck to anything for more than a day or two. However, I have gone along with some crazes like a juicer (bork), a smoothie maker (yum), a nutribullet (undecided). I bought cook books on health eating and meal ideas (Joe Wicks is a GOD).

The thoughts were in my head that I needed to do something but when it came to it, my brain just would not let me do it. I looked at things as too much of a faff on, a chore almost. Now, I look back and think how is preparing healthy food to nourish my body a chore? I just had to find a way to enjoy it.

I had to work on so many other factors as always my mindset was the main one. Once I knew I had a mental illness, I was able to stop being so hard on myself. I am holistic, so I looked for ways to combat this through my nutrition.

I had then convinced my brain that I was okay

exactly how I was, and said it enough times until I believed it. My stomach is the only area I am conscious of (but I did house two massive babies inside).

The rest I can deal with. I personally believe this view was not healthy for me because it meant I would eat whatever I wanted and not care just because 'I was happy with my body'. Instead, I needed to be thinking about how I was treating my body. It took some work to retrain my brain to think a new way again, which was ten times harder when dealing with all of the drama in my life, so my mental health took a huge knock in the process, too. It all became mentally exhausting, which left me physically exhausted as a result.

Skip to the present day and because I learnt so much about mindset and have an appreciation for me as a person and a brush with death in terms of an abnormal smear which resulted in a very large area of pre-cancer cells being removed while I was under general anesthesia, I realized I needed to be taking much better care of my body. I needed to stop talking so much and actually put the words in to action.

I went vegan at one point and it felt good, but as with most things in my past life it never lasted long. Why did it not last long? I believe it was because I had not worked fully on getting my mind in a healthy space, i.e. dealing with my mental health issues.

However, I love the thought of only eating fresh and cutting out all the rubbish that is put in food nowadays. So, although I am not a vegan, I admire them and as with everything, each to their own. If they are happy, so am I.

Now I am aware of how my mind works, and when I know I am having doubts or 'down days' I am more consciously aware. I tell myself 'you're having a down day, don't eat the junk it will make you feel worse. Go for a walk, have a drink of juice (sweetness), have some fruit'.

So many ways to occupy my brain to stop it overthinking and going down a negative path. It's all been a learning process on what works for me personally, not listening to what works for others, assuming it will work for me. Sometimes it will, most of the time it won't, but you never know if you don't try.

Is it easy? No, not at all. I feel every day is a battle, just some days are easier than others. I feel more confident now that I am eating fresh and clean. I no longer eat any pre made meals.

I eat junk in moderation. I like to make things fresh. I decided that I would remove meat from my diet and slowly remove other categories from my diet until my body and mind were happy. I encourage you to follow a nutrition plan that works for you and you alone.

We are all individuals and we make our own decisions. So many people have an opinion and judge us for our choices and it really infuriates me. Be happy being you.

The other thing I have learnt though the courses I have attended and the people I have spoken to is that each body needs different nutrition plans. Don't just go for the plans in magazines as they are 'generic,' they are not specific to an individual.

What works for one will not necessarily work for another person. It may be too much or too little. You have to find a balance that works well for you.

The foods that are bad for us are not just doing harm on the inside, but mentally too. If you have ever detoxed you will understand, because you feel awful after a few days and your body tries to eliminate toxins from your body.

Junk food makes us lethargic and unhappy after (not during). Eating clean has made me realize a lot of my mental health issues were increased by the food choices I was making that were inhibiting the way I felt.

Even though I mainly eat clean, I do have 'naughty snacks', but these are in moderation because I don't want to go back to feeling ill and unhappy. I choose to enjoy my food in my own way. Being grateful and more thoughtful around my nutritional choices, I find I enjoy food so much more.

I eat slowly and enjoy the moment and in return I feel fuller and more satisfied. Have you ever 'scoffed' a chocolate bar or packet of crisps so fast that you want more? Did you even taste it? Did you enjoy it? Do you feel terrible after?

I remember all those times and how I felt and that itself stops me from doing it again. I don't want to get to a point when my self-talk is constantly negative and I end up punishing myself, and for what? It's a vicious cycle and has the potential to become life threatening, not only mentally and emotionally, but physically.

Don't wait for Monday to start or the first of the month. Make today the day you decide to decide to make the change. You owe it to yourself, to your body, to your friends and family to be around as long as you can. After all, there is so much to live for if you choose to see it.

Quotes

'Let food be thy medicine and medicine be thy food.'
~ Hippocrates

'The doctor of the future will no longer treat the human frame with drugs, but rather will cure and prevent disease with nutrition.'
~ Thomas Edison

'Your diet is a bank account. Good food choices are good investments.'
~ Bethenny Frankel

'Your health and happiness are important, so stand strong.'
~ James Duigan

'Every time you eat is an opportunity to nourish your body.'
~ Unknown

Did you know?

- Avocados have twice as much potassium as a banana.

- Broccoli contains twice the vitamin C of an orange and almost as much calcium as whole milk.

- Fermented foods such as yogurt, sauerkraut and miso are a good probiotic bacteria and help the gut stay healthy.

- A number of studies confirm that we should never shop when hungry as we buy the wrong foods. Always take a list (and try to stick to it).

- Enjoying food encourages you to eat slow. That way you digest food better and can feel fuller quicker therefore meaning you eat less.

- Drinking water with a meal aids digestion and nutrient absorption and keeps your digestive tract lubricated therefore possibly preventing constipation and bloating.

Putting it into practice

- Educate yourself on what works best for you, listen to your body and get a feel for how your body looks and changes.

- ❖ Never shop when hungry, you will end up buying more food. Find something to eat first then go shopping.

- ❖ Never eat when stressed, you will release more cortisol and also you will eat quicker therefore possibly eat more than you would, make the wrong choices and feel regret after.

- ❖ Meal prep, plan meals for a few days and make a shopping list for only those days.

- ❖ Stock healthy snacks for when you're tempted to eat, try having a drink of water first (you may just be dehydrated)

- ❖ You made it a habit so you can change it to a new habit, small goals first, don't restrict yourself too much.

Visit www.attunedmindset.co.uk to find hints and tips on eating the healthy way that works for you and ensure you start as you mean to go on.

What have you taken from this chapter?

What one thing will you implement going forward?

....
....
....
....
....
....
....
....
....
....
....
....
....
....
....
....
....
....
....
....
....
....

Notes

Chapter 9: Never Stop Learning

'A child without education, is like a bird without wings.'
~ Tibetan proverb

What is Education?

So, the dictionary states that education is:
1. The process of receiving or giving systematic instruction, especially at a school or university.

2. An enlightening experience.

The second one is the one I prefer. The word education is actually derived from the Latin word 'Educate', which means to train or to mold.

The key to educating yourself is being able to understand what method is most effective for you. However, most teachers have set ways of teaching which are not the same for all students. Therefore, it is essential you know how you learn so you can then ask the teacher to explain things in a different way that you are able to understand and ultimately learn.

Learning styles are evolving all the time. Initially, it was only Visual, Auditory and Kinesthetic, however more have been added.

> - Visual (Spatial) - You prefer using pictures, images.
> - Auditory (Oral) - You prefer using sound and music.
> - Kinesthetic (Physical) - You prefer using your body, hands and doing.
> - Verbal (Linguistic) - You prefer using words, both speech and writing.
> - Logical (Mathematical) - You prefer to use logic, reasoning and systems.
> - Social (Interpersonal) - You prefer to learn in groups or with other people.
> - Solitary (Intrapersonal) - You prefer to work alone and use self-study.

So, why educated yourself? Well, it's nothing new! Back in the late sixteenth century, Francis Bacon stated 'Knowledge is power.' With this in mind, that is why we need to educate ourselves.

We are constantly learning every single day. Have you ever heard something and then used the phrase 'you learn something new every day.'? I'm sure you have at some point, even if it's something you're not that interested in learning.

Learning is not only necessary for life, it's important we continue to keep learning in order to keep our brain active. A friend of mine whom I admire a lot told me 'Education is the act of training the conscious mind to become subconscious' ~ *Steven.*

It took a while to process this perspective, but it's so true. For example, once you learn to ride a bike, you get to a point where you don't even have to think about it, the same with driving. When we learn something new, we then put it in our subconscious ready for when we consciously need to retrieve it.

You are never too old to learn. Make today the day you decide that education matters and you're willing to expand your mind and knowledge.

When we choose a subject to study that we have an interest in we become more engaged. What we learn goes into our memory. Our brain builds the memory. First, your brain encodes the message- if we don't encode the message we can forget it.

Then, our brain consolidates the information so it can be retrieved. The best way to keep information in your brain is to keep retrieving it to strengthen the neural pathway. Guess how else you can help your memory?

Sleep well, eat well (nutrients to help the brain preform), exercise (oxygen to the brain) and finally, challenging your brain (learning new things to keep you mentally active). The brain is fascinating and as with the rest of our body, we need to do all that we can to protect it, nourish it and keep it active.

Learning is essential not only for the brain but so that we can build upon our knowledge. Once we have learnt something we must not stop there. As most of you will be aware, things are changing constantly in the world around us and we need to be able to adapt so much quicker.

Technology is advancing. I remember having a mobile phone for a few years but now you're lucky if you have the same one for more than a year without changing to a newer model or a completely different model! Either way, we need to begin to learn how to use the new version.

Even with updates we have to adapt to change and learn how the new system works. We continuously need to learn, and in doing so we need to be able to adapt our brains to store the correct information- a bit like updating the software idea, we need to update our brain with new information.

Sometimes, we often try to cram in too much information and our brain struggles to cope and often forgets things because you never spend enough time 'encoding' the message on. Another reason why we need to slow down our pace, breathe and be in the present moment.

Why should be keep learning:
1. To keep relevant
2. To add to your list of attributes/profile
3. Ignite new ideas/plans
4. Open your mind, changing your perspective
5. Pay it forward- pass on your knowledge

To be successful in life we must be willing to learn. There is no harm in learning something that has the potential to become useful in your life. Learning happens every day without us realizing, so imagine what you could learn if you began to become aware.

My experience

At school I was always a trier from reception and onwards. I always remember that I really wanted to do my work well and impress people. 'Oh well, I tried'- this thought was what I got fixed in my head.

All I would ever be is a trier. No matter how I tried, I would always be told I could do better, but how can I do better than my best? This lead to thinking 'What's the point in trying, I will never be *good enough.*' I was average in all my classes and subjects, meaning I was not in the lower sets for those who needed extra support and I was not in the top sets with the 'swats'- clever kids.

Yet I wanted to be in the top set, but as mentioned before, my own fears and limitations seemed to pull me back and I settled for not being 'good enough' to join the so called swats.

My comments in my reports were always, 'Abigail tries hard but is easily distracted'. No one ever tried to stop the distractions other than shout at me to concentrate. It was true, mind, but I always thought it was others distracting me and being the fool I was, I let them, and I would be the one who got caught!

I just found it hard to concentrate and I still do. My mind is forever wandering. Also, it was a good indication that I always wanted to follow the crowd and be liked, to be a cool kid.

Oh how I wish I could go back and tell myself that education mattered more than trying to fit in with people who are not likeminded. All they wanted was to mess around and deep down I didn't. I wanted to be a 'swat', a clever kid, but I never gave myself the chance, nor did I feel anyone believed it was a possibility. I just felt average, nothing special.

I struggled with secondary school too when the work went up on the difficulty scale, yet I remained in middle sets. I just could not get my head around some of the work.

It seemed to confuse me. I often needed things explaining again and again until I either understood or gave up asking because I was embarrassed that I had not understood. I always remember my English teacher saying that she understood my work because she knew me, but anyone else reading it would not.

Maybe someone should have checked me for learning disorders at this point? It would have helped a huge amount and stopped me feeling so 'stupid'. However, this was not the case and I went undiagnosed until I was 28 and I decide to get checked myself when I enrolled for an Open University Psychology degree.

I had done previous courses prior to this and never given it much thought, just labeled myself as average and 'muddled through'. The diagnosis is in no way an excuse in my eyes, it has simply helped me to understand my way of thinking in terms of learning.

I have adapted and found ways that work for me. I am also not afraid to tell people that I have dyslexia and that I need things explaining in a different way. When I say things that come out muddled I don't care anymore, I know my brain is just 'having a moment'.

One thing I always prided in myself in is my common sense. Granted , sometimes it's warped but hey, it's part of my character and therefore part of me, (or crazy mamma, as I like to label it with the kids who always point out when I get things muddled). I have an illogical way of figuring things out. I was pleased to have mystified the examiner when I did the test for dyslexia.

I came out diagnosed with mild dyslexia and this was due to me being able to perform some of the tasks, albeit not in the usual logical way, but I did them nonetheless, so he had to mark it as a pass.

Turns out after years of just 'coping', I have made my own methods that work for me and now am a full time University Student and having faith in myself has got me through my first year with no re-sists and slightly better than average ranking.

I have always wanted to better myself and deep know I have known that there is more in me to give in an academic sense. Initially, before my children when I was 22, I decided I wanted to go to University and set my sights on Nottingham Trent and even visited the university and accommodation.

I went back to college and did my access to higher education to gain entry. I was accepted and I was super proud, not only because I was clever enough to go to university but because I gained a distinction in Maths compared to my 'D' at GCSE level where I thought I was 'thick'. On reflection, I put it down to not being supported enough at school, in terms of the way it was being taught simply made no sense to me.
At college, however, the teacher was amazing and he gave me a different way of thinking and it actually made sense. The fact that I learn in a different way does not make me 'thick' or 'less clever' than anyone else, the fact is we all learn in different ways.

I still face these issues today but I just tell my teacher/lecturer to explain it in another way and to clarify my understanding. Personally, I like analogies. In fact, I love them. If I can help make a story from the information then it sticks better.

We all have our own ways and we should not be made to feel less adequate than any other person. If you want to learn then it is your right to ask for it to be delivered to you in a way that best suits your needs. The truth is that we are all unique and we should embrace it, not be ashamed of it.

Writing this book proved to be a challenge. I was able to see just how my dyslexia affects me. I write in the same way that I talk. Now I have realized just how bad my articulation is. I must admit, now I am aware of it, as with everything else, I am able to work on it and improve.

I now don't ever want to stop learning. I love expanding my brain, even if the majority of it does not save to my mental memory stick. I wholeheartedly believe each person we meet has something to teach us, even if we don't agree. You're never too old to learn, either. I felt slightly awkward being 31 and returning to university with the youth of today, fresh out of college.

That being said, I actually found some great friends. I know, I said friends... I'm a changed person in more ways than one! I went without fear of talking to people. I love listening to their stories- all the time I am learning, mainly about how the youth of today live, which makes me smile (yes, I know 32 is not old, but it's older than 18). I'm not old by any means but it's funny when you say something and they are like 'OMG, what?' Or I say something and get it wrong like 'MEME' (mem mey).

How wrong was I! Before I would have been, like, 'ground, you may open and swallow me up', but I laughed it off and said that I have never actually heard someone say the word-now I know (always learning).

I also use my children as a way of learning, I am really interested in what they have learnt and we have reflection time just before bed. We talk about our day and what we have learnt. If something was challenging, we talk about what we need to do to make it better.

With children their brains work slightly differently and I wish it never changed and, to some extent, I still have a childlike mentality. They are so curious and amazed by life, I love the look of wonder in their eyes, their ability to explore and expand their minds. To watch them grow and learn to hold things, feed themselves, crawl, walk, talk, and mimic you (not my favorite part but it helps me learn). They are fascinating creatures. I have learnt so much from both my children and I am thrilled that I get to keep watching them learn and grow every day.

Reading is a great learning resource I use. It's mainly audio I use but it's all learning. I actually found that I learnt more with audio while I was driving. I really encourage my children to read and we have story time.

I feel it helps them to communicate better and use language to express their feelings. They are more imaginative and they gain the ability to pick up anything and be able to read it. It's empowering to watch.

I google a lot. I mean, who doesn't these days!

I even have my Dad on 'OK, Google' which is very entertaining. (Just don't google symptoms as you're almost certain that it will tell you you're about to die! Use the actual NHS site for that stuff).

I know that even after my degree, I am always going to be on some course or another related to what I love or just something that I find interesting. We should never stop learning and never feel we know everything as this is just unrealistic and impossible.

Quotes

'No matter what people tell you, words and ideas can change the world.'
~ Robin Williams

'I have no special talent. I am only passionately curious.'
~ Albert Einstein

'The capacity to learn is a gift; the ability to learn is a skill; the willingness to learn is a choice.'
~ Brian Herbert

'Tell me and I forget. Teach me and I remember. Involve me and I learn.'
~Benjamin Franklin

Did you know?

- According to a study in 2009 they found that our brain does not have the capacity to multitask on two concurrent goals simultaneously. (Charron and Koechlin, 2010)

- Napping after learning can increase memory retention- (Read, 2011)

- Our brain prefers images over text (Medina, 2014)

- Constantly looking at the world through smart phones may results in us trusting them to store the information for us. – 'The google effect'

- The brain makes up about 2% of a human's body weight.

- The brain contains about 100 billion neurons (nerve cells).

- The brain is only capable of surviving 5-6 minutes if it does not get oxygen, after which it dies.

Putting it into practice

- ❖ Find the way you learn best- see my website for a link to a test.

- ❖ Find something you love and make a point of learning more about it.

- ❖ Educate yourself on things that mean something to you, don't rely on other people, and find out for yourself.

- ❖ Live life full of curiosity and find ways to fulfil that curiosity.

Visit www.attunedmindset.co.uk to find motivational tools to ensure you start as you mean to go on.

What have you taken from this chapter?

What one thing will you implement going forward?

Notes

Chapter 10: The power of thoughts

'Change your thoughts and you change your world.'
~ Norman Vincent Peale

Thoughts

The definition of Thoughts:
1. An idea or opinion produced by thinking, or occurring suddenly in the mind.
2. The action or process of thinking.

Our thoughts are more powerful than we often realize. They determine our mood and emotions.

We're not that good at controlling our thoughts, as we often get distracted. Our brain is made of neurons, 100 billion of them. We can think about things that our not really in front of us- our imagination. It is subconscious brain activity. It is still one of the biggest mysteries. So, how do we gain control?

Sometimes, in order to think clearly, we need to quieten the mind by removing unnecessary thoughts which are often distracting. Although they occur subconsciously, we still have the power to control them.

It links back to most of the chapters in this book. We need to educate ourselves on how to better deal with our thoughts. We need to listen and acknowledge. We need to appreciate and be grateful for our body and our mind. We need to look after it. Overall, we need to take care of ourselves and take time out.

At the end of the day, our thoughts are simply thoughts until we choose to turn them into actions. This is where the power of choice comes from. We often fight with our thoughts, sometimes thinking out loud is an option (depending on the thoughts - be wise).

Introduce the term mindfulness into your life. In doing so you will be able to retrain your mind and in turn rewire your brain to a new way of thinking. It also helps you focus on your breathing and makes you more aware of the situation, circumstances and reality. It's all too easy for us to recall bad, negative thoughts because we put so much emphasis on them.

Try switching this to good, positive thoughts and see the difference it can make in your life. If you look hard enough, there will be a positive in all situations if you choose to find it.

Practice compassion, empathy, think about how others are feeling, how would you feel? Rather than criticizing ourselves or others, we need to learn new ways to focus our thoughts.

Stephen Hawking once said 'Intelligence is the ability to adapt to change.' We need to open our minds to change, not as a negative but to see the positive. 'One of the basic rules of the universe is that nothing is perfect, perfection simply doesn't exist.

Without imperfection, neither you nor I would exist'. He was a very wise man, so maybe we need to think about this the next time we think we're not good enough or are giving ourselves negative self-talk.

Psychology Today posted a great article in May 2016, titled 'The Power of Positive Self Talk'. They discussed that we have developed negative self-talk through feelings of anger, fear, guilt and hopelessness.

They advise we need to internally 'overwrite' them, however, it is not self-deception, it is 'recognizing the truth in situations and in yourself.' One of the fundamental truths is that you will make mistakes. To expect perfection in yourself or anyone else is unrealistic.'

I myself have experienced Cognitive Behavioral

Therapy (CBT). This is a talking therapy that can help manage problems by changing the way you think and behave. CBT is based on the concept that your thoughts and feelings are interconnected. The aim is to help you deal with overwhelming problems in a more positive way by breaking them down to become more manageable.

CBT is dealing with current problems and you are able to discuss practical ways to improve your state of mind on a daily basis. With the help of your therapist you are able to work out if your thoughts are unrealistic or unhelpful.

You then work on ways to change these thoughts and behaviors. You are then able to take away skills to implement in your life after the course of treatment is finished. It does, however, require you to put the effort in and learn to help yourself cope. Given that you are committed to making change and willing to do what it takes to make the change this is a great option in my opinion.

If CBT is not for you then there are other options to explore such as counselling (talking about your thoughts and feelings and finding solutions) or Mindfulness-based therapies (working on preventing thoughts and feelings from becoming overwhelming).

I once went for an holistic treatment and the therapist advised I should take St John's wort. It is a herbal remedy that has been used for hundreds of years to treat mental health problems. According to Mind it can be used as a remedy to 'treat mild and moderate depression, seasonal affective disorder (SAD), mild anxiety and sleep problems'. It is thought to work in a similar way to standard antidepressant medication due to similar ingredients.

More information can be found via www.mind.org.uk, as I am not a medical professional, I would advise you check full details before considering this remedy as an option.

When we are able to change our thoughts, the world around us starts to change.

My experience

As I have mentioned in Chapter 6, it was only after my mentor and friend Dave told me that only we have the power to control our own thoughts that I began to really stop and think about this for a while. I am a self-confessed over thinker and my thoughts were often my downfall.

I began to look for ways to help control my thoughts and, to be honest, it's like a constant battle and probably always will be due to my mental health conditions. The way I win? It's to be aware of my thoughts and catch them mid-flow. I decide to change them if they will not serve me.

I remember listening to 'The Secret' and it gave the analogy of thoughts being seeds. I love analogies as they make so much more sense to me. I began to think that if the law of attraction is true, which on reflection, I wholeheartedly agree, then are the seeds I keep planting the ones I really want to grow?

Or am I simply planting weeds that will overgrow and kill all my happiness? I'm not a gardener as much as I wish I was, having found a love for nature on my journey to find my own happiness, however I feel I am a gardener of my mind. I ensure I clear the weeds in order to allow the flowers to grow and blossom into something amazing.

Now, I am not saying you can think something

once and it will become a reality, it is the persistence of those thoughts. We normally think negatively. We start off with a bad morning i.e. we sleep in, then the day gets worse, you're stuck in traffic, you get to work late, someone is not happy with you, you forgot your lunch, you left your wallet, now you're annoyed and hungry, you are so busy, it's noisy.

The list can go on and it's because your thoughts are focused on the negatives. Imagine if you could choose to think only positive thoughts? Your day would surely change, right? RIGHT! I put this to practice all the time.

As soon as the negative thought comes into my head I stop, breathe and then decide if it is worth my energy. Remember, it is the persistency of the thoughts that make them a reality, not just one instance of it. If not, I switch my frequency and look for the positive - trust me, sometimes I know it's the hardest thing.

So, my tip is look for something small and simple like you are still breathing. Life is too unpredictable to 'sweat the small stuff' (another really good book). I believe the best way to understand your thoughts is to become in tune with how you are feeling - it's the best indicator of what you're thinking.

You can't feel down in the dumps if you're having positive thoughts and you can't feel elated when having negative thoughts. Due to my mental health I feel I am in a constant battle with my thoughts and some days are harder than others but now I know I am in control and I know I can change them if I fight hard enough.

Over time, this process has become easier and easier and I am now at a point where my brain does the swap automatically. With tips from the other chapters such as breathing and self-care, I am more in tune with myself and I can therefore use self-help to get me through the day.

I still turn to a therapist when I feel my thoughts are too overwhelming, but due to time scales, I find self-help and being aware helps me to be able to cope while waiting to be seen. I always laughed at the Americans who all have therapists but do you know what? I think we should take note and stop feeling like seeing someone is a bad thing.
Talking to a stranger who will listen and not judge is not therapy for me, it's a breath of fresh air. People I know will always have an opinion, it's in our nature, I think, as everyone does it (except trained therapists). Sometimes offloading our thoughts is all we need.

I often talk things over to myself out loud at home or in the car and when I sound it out, it often clears things up. I write it down on paper, then I re-read and rip it up and throw it in the bin. I make lists of what I need to do so my mind is less cluttered.

I like structure so I know what's coming next. Every night as I tuck my children into bed we talk about our day and what the plan is for the next day. It helps them to communicate and remember their day. It helps my mind get a little clarity.

It is only when we realize that only we can control our thoughts, we are the only ones who know how we are feeling. I get annoyed when people say 'oh, I know how you're feeling', inside I'm screaming 'NO, YOU DON'T, HOW COULD YOU?'. I no longer say this as I appreciate where they are coming from in terms of trying to empathize with me.

However, we are all individuals and all our experiences are personal. They may be similar but no one can EVER fully know how the other person is feeling because they are simply not able to know. If I am ever stuck as to how I am feeling I just ask myself - as crazy as it sounds!

I always know the answer so it's not that crazy. I am so lucky that on my journey I was put in the path of an amazing coach called Carol-Anne who invited me to join SNAPP HAPPY and it was with this and their Snapp bands that I knew they had the answer I was looking for.

A tool to help me literally snap out of my negative thought process. I also put on happy dance music when I need to break the negative thought cycle when it is really strong. I force myself to sing in the car and sensibly dance and smile, smiling more at how crazy I must look but I kid you not, all I get is other people smiling at me so there is no harm in making others smile while your simply trying to make yourself smile. It's contagious.

In order to live a life of positivity in a world covered in negativity I have learnt that I must first change my way of thinking. I tune out of the negative things such as the news, I only look for things relevant to my cause.

I unfollow people on social media who only like to complain, moan or be mean to others. I surround myself with likeminded people and I get out in the fresh air and appreciate the word we live in. I choose to see the positives.

Only I have the ability to change my thoughts and ways of thinking. We have the ability to create our own path and I choose a positive one. Our thoughts are the cause and what happens because of our thoughts is an effect, so make sure you're aware of your thoughts and in tune with your emotions.

Follow the other steps in this book and find what works for you to clear your mind to enable you to go to the next chapter and watch your wildest dreams become a reality.

What you think about, you bring about. How? Well, because your brain has switched focus and is noticing the things you are thinking about. You may always pass the same spot and never notice small details but the minute someone points something out you will always notice it.

How many times have you gone somewhere and it is full of people? Did you recognize all of them? What about if you were looking for someone in particular? Once you have focus, you will usually find them because your brain is looking.

Ever wanted to go on holiday then all of a sudden all you see are people going away or adverts? Ever wanted a specific car then they are all you see on the road? Ever spoken about someone you have not seen then a few days later you see them and go 'Hi, I was just saying the other day how I had not seen you in a while!' Strange, but true. You switch your brain onto another frequency.

Our thoughts are just that, OURS! They are personal and of our own making. We have the power to choose what we think and are entitled to our make up our own mind. Let's spend more time focusing on ourselves first to ensure we have a healthy thinking mind ☺

Quotes

'Once you replace negative thoughts with positive ones, you'll start having positive results.'
~Willie Nelson

'May your choices reflect your hopes, not your fears.'
~ Nelson Mandela

'Most folks are as happy as they make their minds up to be.'
~ Abraham Lincoln

'We need to give thought, but we also need to take action. You need to dream without just being a dreamer.'
~ Jim Rohn

Did you know?

- If your brain was a computer it could hold 2.5 million mg.

- We have an average attention span of 20 minutes.

- When intoxicated the brain cannot from memories.
  www.legacybox.com

- Of the thousands of thoughts a person has every day, its estimated that 70% of this mental chatter is negative – self-critical, pessimistic, and fearful.
  www.bebrainfit.com

Putting it into practice

- Remember that our mind has a clever way of convincing us something is true when it isn't. Try writing down your thoughts then you can see them in front of you and decide if they are true.

- Challenge negative thoughts. Take the time to stop and evaluate if they are accurate or even true. Ask yourself if you're assuming the worst, if you are think of all the positive outcomes. Flip your way of thinking.

- Take a break from your thoughts.

Sitting alone in silence going over and over those negative thoughts in your mind is draining and not healthy. Find a way to distract your mind until you're ready to deal with the thoughts as above. Play your favourite music and get up and move around dance. Clean or get on with something you planned to do. Distract yourself for a while.

- ❖ Stop judging yourself. We constantly compare ourselves to others but we are not them and they are not us. Be happy being you. See the positives in yourself. Focus on your strengths.

- ❖ If you are unable to manage your thoughts or they interfere with daily life or your enjoyment in life, please seek professional support. Through counselling and therapy you will be able to work towards a healthy thought process. I did and I hope to help others be strong and seek support without feeling ashamed or embarrassed. It simply means you are choosing to take control of your life and want to live your best life and there is no shame in that.

Visit www.attunedmindset.co.uk to find ways to break out of your thought process and become a positive thinker to ensure you start as you live your best life.

What have you taken from this chapter?

What one thing will you implement going forward?

Notes

Chapter 11: Dream bigger and bolder

'You must be passionate, you must dedicate yourself, and you must be relentless in the pursuit of your goals. If you do, you will be successful.'
~ *Steve Garvey*

<u>Can dreams come true?</u>

The definition of dreams:
1. A series of thoughts, images and sensations occurring in a person's mind during sleep.
2. A cherished aspiration, ambition or ideal.

Of course, my focus is on the second definition. Dreams have the ability to be powerful. They can also come true if you chase them, believing that the can come true.

As a student of psychology, one name comes to mind when I think of dreams - Sigmund Freud. Back in 1899, he published a book called 'The Interpretation of Dreams'. His view was that dreams were forms of 'wish fulfillment', which is the satisfaction of a desire through an involuntary thought process. However, he believed it was all down to interpretation. So, it seems the actual dreams we have when we sleep are subject to interpretation.

That being said, why is it that so many people say 'dreams come true'? Well, I read an article in Psychology Today titled 'Dreams don't come true, they ARE true', a quote from Tony Robbins.

Even the title has me thinking as most dreams are linked to something we has seen, heard or done in the past. It mentioned a study back where pregnant women who had an intuition about the sex of their baby were 70% correct, women who had a dream about the sex were 100% right!

While we are talking about dreams, we might as well discuss sleep. As I have mentioned, we live in a chaotic world where we tend to sleep less. In 2013, a study by the sleep council found that 70% of Britons sleep for 7 hours or less per night, with more than a quarter (27%) experiencing poor quality sleep on a regular basis.

Sleep helps to keep our heart healthy by preventing cortisol from making the heart beat quicker, therefore allowing it to rest, according to a sleep specialist Shalini Paruthi.

According to the NHS, it is advised that in order to get a good sleep, we need to sleep at regular times. Make sure you wind down, make your bedroom sleep friendly and keep a sleep diary. Again, this all relates back to self-care. Sometimes something has to give but not in place of sleep. After all, that's when we get to dream!

Leading nicely back to the subject at hand. So, why dream big? A dream does not just have to be when you are asleep, it can be a day dream. How about looking at dreams as your wildest ambitions? They are the things you always wanted to do, achieve and concur.

Tony Robbins states it best, 'When you feed your mind on a daily basis it creates your experience of life. However, far too many people believe that they 'don't have time' to give their minds the kind of information that can help them create real, concrete results and achieve their dreams.'

Again, this links back to the chapter on education. If we have a dream and want it to happen so badly, we will make the time to educate ourselves on how to go about achieving whatever dream it may be.

It also goes back to thoughts and having the faith in ourselves to chase the dream and make it a reality, telling yourself that it is possible and giving ourselves positive self-talk.

Winner of the Best Law of Attraction Program

2014, Sage Taylor Kingsley-Goddard, published an article for Consiouslifenews.com.

The article stated the brain's part in terms of the law of attraction. We set our mind on a new frequency and focus on where our thoughts are. Through my research I found similar information.

There are many brainwaves, although only one of them will be dominant at any given moment. According to research, there are two states which are most crucial for manifestation and Law of Attraction- Alpha (8-12 Hz Awaken yet relaxed, light mediation) and Theta (4-8 Hz Creativity, Intuition, Hypnotic state, Receptive). Alpha helps to keep us relaxed and calm and Theta enables us to be creative.

Steve Jobs said 'Have the courage to follow your heart and intuition. They somehow already know what you truly want to become. Everything else is secondary'.

I found there are three rules to achieving and making dreams a reality:
1 Think deep enough- to a subconscious level
2. Think high enough- attuning your energy field
3. Think long enough- consistency and support

'The Secret' by Rhonda Bryne is a whole book dedicated to the law of attraction and does a wonderful job of explaining and backing up the reasons why. It really does make sense once you educate yourself with an open mind.

She states 'The Law of Attraction is a law of nature'. It is as impartial and impersonal as the law of gravity is. It is precise and it is exact. Rhonda went and did a whole load of research in to this and I would urge you to listen to the audio, watch the film (Netflix has it) or read the book. It really is fascinating.

It may seem like this chapter has jumped around in subject but tying it all together is the knowledge that if we dream big enough, believe in ourselves and educate ourselves we can make anything possible.

We just have to set ourselves on the right path and the law of attraction will put the rest in to play. There is no need to know how, just know it will happen. It has for me and it is astonishing that I have never known all this before, hence the book so I can share it with others.

By following all the steps in this book which all link to each other you are set to have the most amazing life once you allow yourself to do so.

A quote by Ellen Johnson Sirleaf sticks heavily in my mind. 'If your dreams do not scare you, they are not big enough.' – See what I mean! They all link (fear) so please take on board all that I have shared with you in the book and hey, if it doesn't work for you, that's okay, at least you tried.

What's the worst that could happen? Well, I know what the best is, and that is that you go on to enjoy the rest of your life and make the most of it all in your amazing bubble of positivity and love for life.

My experience

I am a big dreamer always have been and always will. I mentioned before I was a sleeping princess. However, that was just to escape reality and enter a magical world of fantasy in my head where I lived another life, not healthy trust me.

Instead, I should have been facing my reality and removing obstacles and aiming to make the dreams a reality. All well and good saying that now but if only you could go back and give the younger version some friendly advice.

Anyway, the past is the past and it can't be rewritten. So, on with the future and the only difference now is I have the upmost pleasure in seeing so many come true before my own eyes and it is magical. Even having kids was a dream and that came true, twice!

When I first came across making dreams come true, it was through the networking marketing group I was involved with and they talked about this thing called a 'vision board'. You may well have heard of one, they are becoming a popular resource.

You get a board and print off and stick on anything that you would love to have. You can write words on there too. I picked things like holidays, financial freedom, an Audi, a new house, a new watch, self-employment, motivational speaking, write a book and so on.

It's all about making things visual. I would see them and get excited, this was the outcome/reward for my hard work. I have already gained a few, some are just around the corner.

Take writing this book, for example. I always wanted to write a book and I am in no way a writer! I began with doing motivational posts on my social media outlets on a morning to inspire others to have a good day. Then, I went on and wrote some blogs.

The feedback was positive so I decided that after all the drama in my life, I would write a book, but I'd make it a novel using a pen name. I planned the cover, the contents and then looked at self-publishing, then more of life's drama came my way and the book got pushed to the back of my to do list.

It was not until I joined the Female Success network that I was introduced to Authors and Co. We connected straight away and I followed them on social media and after each post I saw I was more and more drawn to the idea of writing a book.
After a single phone call, my book had taken a new form and my name was going on the front as the author. To think that I am currently writing this to be published and having people read it is one dream that makes me super emotional to see become a reality. The key is not to become fixated on the how, just know it's what you want and it will come if you have

the courage to pursue it.

Another example is my car. I always wanted an Audi. I went to the show room and walked away the proud owner of my very own Audi! I'm still not sure how it happened but it did. My house, again, no idea how a single mum of one could afford a mortgage on her own but I did.

The biggest dream which has taken time to manifest is going to University. Initially, after circumstances prevented me from going when I was 22, I thought it would be okay, I could go another year when finances were available.

Then, I became pregnant and that dream seemed to fade into non-existence. However, after she was born I was keen to get my degree to provide a better future for our family. I did it online, then that went fine for two years, even timing my son's birth perfectly without realizing it.

During my third year was when my world was turned upside down from the break up. I then gave up all hope and said I would do it when the kids were in secondary school. Due to childcare circumstances changing, I made a rash decision to quit work and go to University full-time while being a single mum, and just under a one hour commute each way. Hey, it worked and I completed my first year, so dreams do come true and it's not always easy, but it's possible.

Do you think J K Rowling should have given up after twelve publishers turned down Harry Potter? If she did not follow her dreams then Harry Potter would not be the pheromone it is today and will continue to be.

Do you think Walt Disney should have given up the first time he went bankrupt? If he did... I can't even bear to think of a life without Disney, so I won't go there, but you get my point.

It's the one thing I have learnt, more so from watching others, and it links in with fear. It also links to our thoughts and the negative self-doubt when we talk ourselves out of our dreams! I used to be the biggest destroyer of my dreams! Now, I fight with all I have to ensure they come true.

Quotes

'All our dreams can come true, if we have the courage to pursue them.'
~ Walt Disney

'The very substance of the ambitious is merely the shadow of a dream.'
~ William Shakespeare

'The interpretation of dreams is the royal road to a knowledge of the unconscious activities of the mind.'
~ Sigmund Freud

'Dreams at first seem impossible, then seem improbable, and finally, when we commit ourselves, become inevitable.'
~ Mathatma Gandhi

'The biggest adventure you can ever take is to live the life of your dreams.'
~ Oprah

Did you know?

- 1 % sleep more than 9 hours
  7% sleep 8.01-9 hours
  7% sleep less than 5 hours
  22% sleep 7.01-8 hours
  30% sleep 6.01-7 hours
  33% sleep 5-6 hours
  : The Great British bedtime report

- Dreams are said to be inspirational for inventors such as:
  Elias Howe- *The Sewing Machine*
  Dimitri Mendeleyev- *The periodic table*
  Larry Page- *The idea for Google*

- Sleep paralysis occurs between stages of wakefulness and sleep. It feels 100% real and consists of the inability to move or talk, while being completely aware. The amygdala is sent into over drive (terror).

- You can dream up to seven different dreams per night depending on how many REM (Rapid Eye Movement) cycles you have. With the average person dreaming 1-2 hours every night.

Putting it into practice

- ❖ Make a vision board and put on all your dreams. Make sure you add details, e.g. if it's a car- put the make, model, color, interior anything that you want really visualize this. Then dream about it, day dream about it and forget about the how.

- ❖ Don't be afraid of your dreams, if you want it to be a reality then note it down and begin to plan what it would take to make it happen.

Visit www.attunedmindset.co.uk to find ways to make your dreams become a reality and ensure you start as you mean to go on.

What have you taken from this chapter?

What one thing will you implement going forward?

Notes

You made it to the end! Thank you so much and I hope you have taken something positive from the book if not more.

I wrote this book in order to share some of my knowledge on how I ended up becoming more beautiful for being broken.

Did I want to have a hospital stay after by body decided to scare the life out of me? No! However, I am thankful I did because it was the wakeup call I needed.

I don't want others to have to get to breaking point to make changes. The points I make in the book are all things that can be easily achieved by anyone.

So, as a refresher, all you need to do it take some time out and listen to your body and your mind and rediscover who you are (if you already know... KEEP DOING YOU!)

1. BE GRATEFUL
2. REMEMBER TO BREATHE
3. PRACTICE SELF CARE
4. LEAVE YOUR COMFORT ZONE
5. FACE YOUR FEAR
6. EXERCISE DOING WHAT YOU LOVE

7. **EAT THE RAINBOW**
8. **EDUCATE YOURSELF**
9. **THINK POSITIVE THOUGHTS**
10. **DREAM BIG AND ACHIEVE THEM**

For more information or to contact Abigail direct please visit
www.attunedmindset.co.uk